T0247207

The Four Guns

The Stolen History of the Assassinated Presidents

The Four Guns

The Stolen History of the Assassinated Presidents

John Koerner

London, UK
Washington, DC, USA

CollectiveInk

First published by Chronos Books, 2024
Chronos Books is an imprint of Collective Ink Ltd.,
Unit 11, Shepperton House, 89 Shepperton Road, London, N1 3DF
office@collectiveinkbooks.com
www.collectiveinkbooks.com
www.chronosbooks.com

For distributor details and how to order please visit the 'Ordering' section on our website.

Text copyright: John Koerner 2023

ISBN: 978 1 80341 607 6
978 1 80341 616 8 (ebook)
Library of Congress Control Number: 2023941637

All rights reserved. Except for brief quotations in critical articles or reviews, no part of this book may be reproduced in any manner without prior written permission from the publishers.

The rights of John Koerner as author have been asserted in accordance with the Copyright, Designs and Patents Act 1988.

A CIP catalogue record for this book is available from the British Library.

Design: Lapiz Digital Services

UK: Printed and bound by CPI Group (UK) Ltd, Croydon, CR0 4YY
Printed in North America by CPI GPS partners

We operate a distinctive and ethical publishing philosophy in all areas of our business, from our global network of authors to production and worldwide distribution.

Contents

For Heather

Foreword

What would the United States of America be today if Abraham Lincoln, James Garfield, William McKinley, and John F. Kennedy had survived assassination? Would that country, and the world we live in today, be better or worse? It is a daunting question. What if Lincoln and McKinley lived through their second terms? What if Garfield and Kennedy completed their four years in office, instead of both being cut short in their youth, and went on to be reelected?

This book will have three purposes. First, I will explain the circumstances surrounding the four assassinations. One of the books that I authored is titled *Why the CIA Killed JFK and Malcolm X: The Secret Drug Trade in Laos*. I will draw partly from this for the Kennedy assassination, and for some points about Lee Harvey Oswald that are relevant. For the McKinley assassination, I will partly draw from *The Secret Plot to Kill McKinley*, another book that I authored. What is unique about my approach to all four of these assassinations is that I will examine credible evidence of a conspiracy. I do this reluctantly. The word "conspiracy" has a negative connotation, even though many political assassinations in history are often the work of more than one person. They typically take extensive planning, preparation, and organization. The people involved in these assassinations are long since dead. There is no reason to hide from the truth. Think of the new information that has come forward regarding the Robert Kennedy and Malcolm X assassinations, proving extensive plots to kill these men. The information in this book has never been put forward by any other historian regarding the McKinley and Garfield assassinations. I will also be bringing to light new evidence that has come forward since the publication of *The Secret Plot to Kill McKinley*.

To be clear, there is a crucial difference between conspiracy theories and conspiracy facts. Conspiracy theories are about JFK Jr being alive, or the world being flat. I will never associate myself with such nonsense. When I present evidence for a conspiracy it is based on facts, not theories or conjecture. It really is shameful that mainstream historians have to feel stigmatized if they want to venture into this area in a scholarly way, which is my approach. I feel my book may be excluded from mainstream acceptance because I am willing to examine this subject using a fact-based approach. My response is that I am not going to censor myself. The pursuit of the truth is important so that we can find out what really happened on those tragic days. Let the chips fall where they may. Readers can judge for themselves.

The second purpose of this book is to trace the history of the four weapons used in the four assassinations. The reader will find out what types of firearms were used, how the assassins acquired them, and where they are now. Most of this information has never been written about or made public.

The third purpose of this book is to examine how American history would have changed if the presidents had survived the assassinations. To keep this simple, I will treat each president individually. For example, with Garfield, I will extrapolate based on the Lincoln assassination having happened. The same approach will be followed for the others. What would happen at that moment in time moving forward? It is essential to understand just how much these four weapons changed history.

On a personal note, in the foreword for my previous book, I promised I was done with writing. Well, apparently not. I have to say, it is nice to be back.

Part I

The Assassination of President Abraham Lincoln

Chapter 1

The Road to Ford's Theatre

February 18, 1861, was a strange day for the United States. On that day in Montgomery, Alabama, the capital city of the Confederacy, Jefferson Davis was sworn in for a six-year term as President of the Confederate States of America.[1] The southern states had finally seceded from the Union and formed their own country. President-Elect Abraham Lincoln was touring the northern states seeking advice and goodwill for his upcoming administration. On February 18, 1861, Lincoln was in Albany, New York, the state capital. He was greeted by local politicians and journalists. These included Albany's Democratic Mayor George Thacher, who met Lincoln at the train station; Thurlow Weed, State Republican Chairman, and editor of the *Albany Evening Journal*; Republican Governor Edwin D. Morgan; Republican US Senator Ira Harris; and Democratic Congressman Erastus Corning, who was hosting Lincoln, his wife, and their three children.[2]

As the presidential procession headed down Broadway and turned up State Street, there were two people in the cheering crowd who would meet years later in the fateful box in Ford's Theatre where Lincoln was shot on April 14, 1865. The first was Clara Harris.[3] Born in Albany on September 9, 1834, she was the daughter of prominent New York Senator Ira Harris.[4] Clara was engaged to her stepbrother Henry Rathbone, who later served with distinction in the battles of Antietam and Fredericksburg.[5] While living in Washington, D.C., with her family, on the corner of 15th and H Streets, Clara became a prominent member of the Washington social elite. She was friends with Mary Todd Lincoln, often dining at the White House with her, and accompanying her to the theater.[6] On April 14, 1865, Harris and her fiancé

Henry accepted a last-minute invitation to see *Our American Cousin* with the president and the first lady at Ford's Theatre. After the president absorbed the fatal head shot, Rathbone unsuccessfully attempted to prevent the shooter from escaping. The assassin stabbed Rathbone with a Bowie knife, leapt from the box, landed on the stage awkwardly, and fractured his leg.[7]

The person who landed on that stage, John Wilkes Booth, was also in the crowd that day in Albany on February 18, 1861. Booth watched from outside Stanwix Hall where he had been staying. This was at the corner of Maiden Lane and Broadway. Half a block down Broadway, Lincoln was headed to the Delavan House, where he would be staying the night.[8] Booth was performing at the Gayety Theatre on Green Street in a play called *The Apostate*. He had fallen on his dagger a few days before during a performance and nearly killed himself.[9] Booth was confined to the Stanwix until he could recover enough to resume his acting duties, giving him a chance to see Lincoln pass the hotel. After seeing Lincoln, Booth grew increasingly bitter, and talked openly against Lincoln in the bar at the Stanwix. Booth started railing against Lincoln and the Union to the point where the treasurer for the Gayety told him he had better keep his mouth shut or it would discourage attendance.[10] Booth decided for now to hold his tongue.

He had other problems to worry about, in the form of a married actress he was having an affair with. She was Albany native Henrietta Irving. On April 26, 1861, Irving came to the Stanwix to meet with Booth, but he decided to end the relationship. Irving then grabbed a knife and lunged toward Booth, but he deflected it with his arm, resulting in a slash to his face. Irving then dramatically pretended to commit suicide by cutting herself, but, according to an Albany Police report, "did no real harm."[11]

So, while in Albany, Booth escaped two scrapes with death and openly discussed his hatred for Abraham Lincoln. If this is what he was willing to say publicly against Lincoln in a northern city, imagine the depths of Booth's hatred privately. Albany historian Jack McEneny agrees that Albany may have been the place where assassination started to creep into the mind of John Wilkes Booth.

"Undoubtedly, he was in this crowd somewhere watching this man from Illinois with all of his background and support with anti-slavery, abolitionist forces and you could bet he was seething. And whether that germ of thought of finally eliminating Lincoln from this earth crossed his mind at the time...It may well have started in Albany, New York," said McEneny.[12]

Booth would also be present at another key moment in Lincoln's life. It was the evening of April 11, 1865. It would be Lincoln's final speech. The previous day, crowds at the White House had clamored for the president to give a speech. He asked for a day to prepare. It was late in the evening when journalist and friend Noah Brooks emerged with Lincoln from the second floor of the White House on the North Portico, holding a candle to light up the president's words. Lincoln waited for several minutes for the noise of the crowd to die down. Robert E. Lee had surrendered to Ulysses S. Grant just two days before this,[13] and the country was ready to celebrate. Lincoln, however, had other things on his mind, including how Reconstruction was helping former slaves in Louisiana, and his desire to see the franchise extended to other former slaves:

The amount of constituency, so to speak, on which the new Louisiana government rests, would be more satisfactory to all, if it contained fifty, thirty, or even twenty thousand, instead of only about twelve thousand, as it does. It is also unsatisfactory to some that the elective franchise is not given to the colored man. I would myself prefer that it were now conferred on the very intelligent, and on those who serve our cause as soldiers. Still the question is not whether the Louisiana government, as it stands, is quite all that is desirable. The question is, Will it be wiser to take it as it is, and help to improve it; or to reject, and disperse it? Can Louisiana be brought into proper practical relation with the Union sooner by sustaining, or by discarding her new State government?

Some twelve thousand voters in the heretofore slave-state of Louisiana have sworn allegiance to the Union, assumed to be the rightful political power of the State, held elections, organized a State government, adopted a free-state constitution, giving the benefit of public schools equally to black and white, and empowering the Legislature to confer the elective franchise upon the colored man. Their Legislature has already voted to ratify the constitutional amendment recently passed by Congress, abolishing slavery throughout the nation. These twelve thousand persons are thus fully committed to the Union, and to perpetual freedom in the state—committed to the very things, and nearly all the things the nation wants—and they ask the nation's recognition and its assistance to make good their committal.[14]

Even though it was limited, this was the first time Lincoln publicly endorsed the right to vote for former slaves. Although the plot to kill Lincoln was in place long before that night, Booth had a predictably violent, racist reaction to this speech. "That means nigger citizenship," Booth told fellow conspirator Lewis Powell. "Now, by God, I will put him through. That will be the last speech he ever gives."[15]

Booth had been attempting to kidnap—or kill—Lincoln for several years as an undercover member of the Confederate Secret Service (hereinafter the CSS). This was a clandestine network of spies dedicated to furthering the cause of southern independence. The network stretched from Canada all the way to Confederate President Jefferson Davis in Richmond, Virginia. Booth's fame as an actor allowed him to travel in secret without arousing suspicion. He visited the St. Lawrence Hotel in Montreal, Canada, several times. This was a known contact for Confederate agents to secretly meet with the British government. Confederate Colonel Robert M. Martin and Confederate Colonel James Gordon, both CSS agents, confirmed after the war that they knew and met with Booth in Canada.[16]

Another way to trace Booth's linkages to the CSS was the extensive network of agents set up to ensure that his escape route was successful from Ford's Theatre after he shot Lincoln. One such agent was John Lloyd, who owned Surrat's Tavern, a known Confederate resupplying station for CSS agents. Lloyd hid and fed Booth, along with co-conspirator David Herold. Dr Samuel Mudd, who set Booth's leg, had already recently helped CSS agent Walter Bowie. Thomas Jones, a member of the Confederate Signal Corps, helped Herold and Booth safely cross the Potomac River into Virginia. The Confederate Signal Corps, which answered only to President Jefferson Davis, was a clandestine unit with the purpose of moving people and information from the Union into the Confederacy. Colonel John Hughes, who had taken part in the botched Lincoln kidnapping plot, provided food for Booth and Herold at his farm near Nanjemoy Creek in Maryland. William Rollins, who hid Booth and Herold in his house, was also a member of the Confederate Signal Corps. Also, three Confederate soldiers were waiting for Booth to take him further south before he was captured at Garrett's Farm on April 26, 1865. They were Private Absalom Bainbridge, Private William Jett, and their commanding officer, Lieutenant Mortimer Ruggles. This suggests official orders to place them there to further aid Booth's continued escape into Confederate territory.[17]

What this indicates is that the assassination of Lincoln was planned by people at the highest levels of the Confederate government. They certainly had the motive and the most to gain from this. One key turning point was the failed Dahlgren's Raid in February and March 1864. President Lincoln had issued orders to capture Richmond, burn it, and execute President Jefferson Davis and members of his cabinet.[18] This engendered even more hatred against Lincoln, whom the Confederacy blamed for the war because of his orders to invade the southern states. It also gave justification to use assassination in retaliation.

The most logical thesis put forward to explain the assassination is summarized by historians William Tidwell, James O. Hall, and David Winfred Gaddy:

> The leaders in the Confederate government tried to capture President Lincoln as a hostage, and when that effort failed, they decided to attack Union leaders to disrupt command and control of the Union forces. Events in April 1865 moved so fast that John Wilkes Booth thought that he was acting in accordance with Confederate interests, even though...the actual need for such an action had been obviated by the [surrender of Robert E. Lee].[19]

Booth had already been involved in planning a kidnapping of Lincoln. Booth began in September 1864 "to recruit a team to capture Lincoln. In mid-October he went to Montreal, Canada, where he met Confederate agents who may have played some role in direction of the action part of the plan."[20] President Jefferson Davis felt that capturing Lincoln might make the evacuation of Richmond unnecessary, and cripple Union command and control.[21] So an order was given to attempt to capture Lincoln on March 17, 1865, when the president was set to visit Campbell Military Hospital. Booth and his fellow CSS agents were waiting for hours, but Lincoln never showed up. He had changed his plans at the last minute.[22]

Tidwell, Hall, and Gaddy after years of research summarized their conclusions about the assassination:

> Booth seems to have decided to do the best he could do to carry out his mission as he understood it. Originally expecting Lincoln and Grant to be together at Ford's Theatre, Booth shot the president at about ten o'clock on the night 14 April 1865. At the same time, Lewis Powell attacked Secretary of State William Seward, and George Atzerodt got drunk instead of carrying out his assignment to attack Vice-President Andrew Johnson…[It appears that] the Confederates had the knowledge and technical skill to mount an operation against President Lincoln; that they engaged in a number of activities relating to planning such an operation; that John Wilkes Booth was in contact with known Confederate agents; and the course of the war developed in such a way that an attack on Lincoln was a logical amendment to the original plan…Of all the theories of the assassination this is the one that can be the most strongly supported.[23]

In fact, the reason I wanted to go through this evidence is because of that final statement. Too much time has been spent on the notion that Booth only worked with a small band of idiots whom he coerced. If the Lincoln assassination is treated that way, as it is in all the textbooks that I have encountered in my 15 years of teaching Social Sciences, it puts us in the mindset that other assassinations must be the same. If we can help further the truth that this assassination was planned at the highest levels of the Confederate government, it helps us understand that conspiracies are often based on facts, not theories.

Having then briefly dealt with the basic tenets of the assassination, let us move on to examine the gun that Booth used to change the course of history.

Chapter 2

The First Gun

The gun Booth used was a .44-caliber pistol made by Henry Deringer of Philadelphia. It could be easily concealed in his clothing.[1] It was a single-shot weapon, 5.87 inches in length.[2] With only one shot, Booth had no time to reload. Also, if the gun backfired, he would not have a chance to fire a second shot. Within seconds Rathbone was on him. Booth seems to have been prepared for this possibility. What is not widely known is that he was carrying a second Deringer with him that night. Deringers were so small they usually sold in sets of two.[3] When Booth fell to the stage, the other Deringer fell out of his clothing. He probably had the second gun in case he needed to shoot his way out of the theater. This second gun is now in the possession of Ripley's Believe It or Not Museum in St Augustine, Florida. It was purchased by the museum at an auction in San Francisco for $70,000 on June 1, 1994.[4]

Kurtis Moellmann, the exhibits buyer for Ripley's, is the expert on this weapon that had an equal chance of being the murder weapon. This Deringer was a .36 caliber, making it less powerful.[5] This is likely why Booth did not use that one. According to Moellmann, the unused gun "was recovered the next day by a stagehand, who kept it in his possession for years and years, until it entered a private collection, and then ended up in our collection."[6] For many years it was not clear that Booth had two pistols on him. One was recovered on the stage, and another was recovered in the presidential box.

This from the Ford's Theatre website:

After the assassination, theatre patron William T. Kent found the pistol on the floor of the Presidential Box and turned it over to investigators. The U.S. Army Judge Advocate General's Office used it as evidence in the conspirators' trial in May and June of 1865. Eventually the War Department, today's Department of Defense, displayed the Deringer at its headquarters.

In 1931, General Ulysses S. Grant III, in charge of planning the new Lincoln Museum at Ford's Theatre, asked to display the weapon and other Lincoln assassination artifacts. The Adjutant General of the U.S. Army denied the request, saying:

> The relics should not be displayed to the public under any circumstances, on the theory that they would create interest in the criminal aspects of the great tragedy, rather than the historical features thereof, and would have more of an appeal for the morbid or weak-minded than for students of history...The Lincoln relics should not be placed upon exhibition anywhere.
> —The Adjutant General of the U.S. Army

Eventually, the War Department relented. In 1940, [they] transferred Booth's Deringer and other pieces of evidence from the 1865 conspirators' trial to the National Park Service for display at Ford's Theatre National Historic Site. After further questions about propriety, they first went on display in 1942, when a military tribunal for German saboteurs was taking place nearby. Ford's Theatre has displayed the Deringer since.

The above story of the Deringer's movement from hiding to display is included as a permanent exhibit at Ford's Theatre. If you visit the assassination site, you will find the gun by itself in a glass case. It is in the basement museum, toward the right and to the back. Behind the gun is a painting of Lincoln being shot by Booth, with Mary Todd Lincoln sitting next to the president, and the Rathbones positioned across from the first lady.

The display case inscription reads:

> The Gun that Killed Abraham Lincoln. With a single shot John Wilkes Booth changed the course of American history. The gun he chose was a .44 caliber pistol, made by Henry Deringer of Philadelphia. One shot was all that Booth had. The gun was favored for its small size—it could easily be concealed inside a pocket. It fired a single, round lead ball, weighing nearly an ounce—and was most accurate at close range.

A "modern version of a .44 caliber lead ball" sits imbedded underneath the gun below the glass case.

On the wall next to the exhibit a haunting question is asked: "How should museums display weapons of violence?"[7] Keep in mind that of the four weapons used to kill the presidents, only two can be seen by the public—Lincoln's and McKinley's. In subsequent chapters I will explain why that is not the case for Garfield and Kennedy. I think we should feel fortunate that we can view these guns that killed Lincoln and McKinley. The public needs to understand what these weapons did, and how they changed history. People need to see that history happened with real artifacts, not just pictures in textbooks. Only then can we appreciate the impact that these guns had.

There is no question that at least one pistol was recovered from the presidential box, and it is the one on display at Ford's Theatre. What about the other pistol that Ripley's has? Where did it come from? On September 15, 1901, The [Philadelphia] Inquirer published an article about a man who had possession of this second gun that Booth dropped on the stage after the assassination. This seems to verify its authenticity. George Plowman, an architect who lived at 12 North 50th Street in

Philadelphia, showed the pistol in his home to a reporter for *The Inquirer*. "Here it is," he said to the reporter, pulling it from the "pocket of his waistcoat." Here is the account from *The Inquirer*:

> The weapon is about three and a half or four inches long. It bears the Deringer stamp on the lower part of the barrel and also on the side. The letter "F" is also visible on the stock. On the butt of the handle is a neat silver plate carefully set in, bearing the name "J. Wilkes Booth..."
>
> "Since I became the owner of this historic weapon," continued Mr. Plowman, "I have allowed it to go out my possession only once, and that was when it was photographed by *The Inquirer* a short time ago. It was presented to me by the widow of George K. Goodwin...After shooting President Lincoln, Booth in his desire to escape dropped the weapon on the stage at Ford's Theater. After the excitement attending the shooting had died out the stage carpenter found the pistol and kept it. Subsequently he gave it to manager Goodwin. For many years I was associated in business with Mr. Goodwin and after his death I helped to settle up his estate. Mrs. Goodwin offered me a money consideration for my services, but I declined to accept it. Then she gave me the pistol...She also furnished me with the history of the pistol, which I have since verified, not that I disputed it, but simply to assure myself."[8]

At the time, it was not known that Booth had carried two weapons, so Plowman thought this might have been the murder weapon, but it was not.

So, there is clear evidence that two weapons were recovered. One was in the presidential box recovered by theater patron William T. Kent. The other was recovered on the stage by a carpenter, who later gave the gun to George K. Goodwin.

The name of that man, the theater's chief carpenter, was James J. Gifford.[9]

Do we know anything more about this second gun? According to the Lincoln Discussion Symposium:

> Thinking that it was the murder weapon [Gifford] put it in his pocket, feared turning it in to the authorities and kept his mouth shut. Two years later he showed the pistol to George K. Goodwin (owner of the Walnut Street Theatre in Philadelphia) and told him how he found it. He later gave the Deringer to Goodwin, and when Goodwin died in 1882 the pistol was given to his business partner, George Plowman. Plowman informed the press in 1901. The Deringer Gifford found was smaller than the .44-caliber Deringer used by Booth to shoot Lincoln. It was a .36-caliber Deringer, with a 1.5-inch (3.8 cm) barrel and an overall length of 4 inches (10.1 cm).[10]

Can we confirm that George Plowman had a business in Philadelphia in the late 1800s? Gopsill's Philadelphia City Directory for 1887 under "Planing Mills" listed George Plowman's Company at 1017 Chestnut and Fairmont Ave C N 17th.[11] So that checks out. Plowman had a business in Philadelphia during that time period.

Can we confirm that George K. Goodwin was manager of the Walnut Street Theatre in Philadelphia? On September 2, 1911, the *New York Clipper* published a remembrance of a famous Philadelphia actor named John E. McDonough. He was born on February 22, 1825, in London, and then moved with his family to Philadelphia when he was four years old. His father was a carver and a gilder. In fact, he gilded the Walnut and Chestnut Street theaters where his son would later perform as an adult. His father was a teacher in a section of Philadelphia called the Northern Liberties.[12] This was where the gun that killed Lincoln was manufactured.[13] More on that later. John E. McDonough spent several years in the 1850s acting in Philadelphia theaters, including the Walnut Street Theatre and the Arch Street Theatre,[14] the latter of which was where John Wilkes Booth performed from 1857 to 1858.[15] He also was the business partner of Laura Keene,[16] who at the time was touring the country with her new sensational play *Our American Cousin*.[17] This was the play being performed during the Lincoln assassination.

Most importantly for our purposes here, when McDonough died on February 15, 1882, there was an impressive outpouring of emotion for his long career. The funeral took place on February 17, 1882, in New Jerusalem Church on the corner of Brandywine and Broad Streets in Philadelphia. Nearly every major political and theatrical figure in the city turned out to say goodbye. Among the mourners was "George K. Goodwin, manager of the Walnut Street Theatre, and Chestnut Street Opera House, all of Philadelphia."[18] We also can confirm that Plowman died before his wife. After Plowman passed away, Mrs. Goodwin sold the lease of the Walnut Street Theatre and the Chestnut Street Opera House from his estate, giving ownership to J. Frederick Zimmerman and Samuel F. Nixon.[19]

All aspects of Plowman's story check out. We can conclude, then, that he had possession of Booth's second gun. The only question that remains unanswered is: Why did James J. Gifford give the gun to Goodwin? Was Gifford living in Philadelphia at the time? Tacita Barrera, Archivist Assistant for Ripley's Believe It or Not, has some answers to these questions:

> The Booth pistol happens to be one of my favorite pieces in our whole collection! Ripley's acquired the gun from an auction held by Butterfield & Butterfield in 1994. The history of the gun up until that point is quite fascinating. Walter V. Cunningham, Chief Engraver of the J.E. Caldwell Co. inspected the gun in 1971, and determined that the style

of lettering used in the engravings on the gun was common between 1860–1865, so Booth would have bought the gun between those years.

James J. Gifford, chief carpenter of Ford's Theater, found the gun on the stage on the morning of April 15th, 1865. He didn't hand the gun over to authorities out of fear of being labeled a conspirator in the plot to kill President Lincoln, like other Ford Theater employees. The gun remained in his possession until 1867 when he was hired by George Goodwin, co-owner of the Walnut Street Theater in Philadelphia. He gave the gun as a gift to Goodwin as a thank you for employing him. Goodwin kept the gun until he died in the 1890's, and his wife then gave the gun to George Plowman. Plowman was Goodwin's partner at the Walnut Street Theater. The Deringer stayed with the Plowman's until it was sold to Hamilton Cochran in 1971. Plowman actually went public about his possession of the gun in 1901 after the McKinley assassination...[20]

There was also some question about the authenticity of the gun on display in Ford's Theatre. In 1997, there was speculation that the gun had been replaced with a replica by a Northeastern crime syndicate sometime in the 1960s. The Federal Bureau of Investigation (FBI) Crime Laboratory in Washington DC was called in to test the Deringer. Here are the results from the FBI website:

The lab's assignment? To determine beyond a reasonable doubt whether the Deringer pistol displayed at Ford's Theatre was the same pistol pictured in pre-1960s historical photographs of the gun.

Let the tests begin. After a National Park Police captain hand-carried the firearm from Ford's Theatre the half-block to FBI Headquarters—where our lab was then located—the lab's Firearms-Toolmarks Unit conducted a series of physical analyses of the pistol, comparing it to other pistols of similar style and caliber. Because its age and historical value precluded test-firing it, a dental material was used to make a cast of the inside of the barrel and other internal parts. Meanwhile, the lab's Special Photographic Unit superimposed images of the Deringer on historical photographs.

The results? Physical examination revealed a number of imperfections to the display pistol that were unique to the firearm. The most significant was a major crack in the forestock of the gun, which bore evidence of previous repair. The cast of the barrel revealed a counterclockwise rifling (or left twist), which was unusual for that make of gun.

Photographic superimpositions using the Deringer pistol and images from the 1930s demonstrated a close correspondence between them, with unique characteristics such as the crack in the stock, swirl patterns in the grain of the stock, and pit marks on the barrel visible in both.

These and other comparisons led the lab to conclude that the Deringer pistol displayed at Ford's Theatre is the real thing, which you can still see there today.

Case closed.[21]

With the authenticity of both Deringers no longer in doubt, the important questions that remain unanswered are: Where and when did John Wilkes Booth purchase these Deringers? Ford's Theatre offers no answers to these questions. Major biographies of Booth also do not provide the answer. These include *American Brutus: John Wilkes Booth and the Lincoln Conspiracies* by Michael W. Kauffman (Random House, 2004);

Fortune's Fool: The Life of John Wilkes Booth (Oxford University Press, 2015) by Terry Alford; and William Tidwell's *Come Retribution: The Confederate Secret Service and the Assassination of Lincoln* (Barnes and Noble, 1998). Ripley's Believe It or Not also does not know when Booth bought the gun in its possession. When I asked if the museum had any evidence for that date, Barrera responded:

> Unfortunately no, having some sort of receipt or proof of purchase would really help solidify our story though. The 1860–1865 range is the closest we have for the time he bought it. One would assume Booth didn't buy the gun and engrave his name in the handle right before he assassinated Lincoln, but I wouldn't put it past him.[22]

So, where and when did John Wilkes Booth buy these two guns? Is it possible to find out? The answer is yes, if we follow the right breadcrumbs.

Chapter 3

Northern Liberties

If we are going to build a case for where John Wilkes Booth bought the gun to commit the first presidential assassination in United States history, Philadelphia seems like the most obvious place to start. The closest member of his family, his sister Asia Booth Clarke, lived at the corner of 13th and Callowhill Streets.[1] Born on November 19, 1835, Asia was the eighth child of Mary Ann and Junius Booth. In 1859 she married actor John Sleeper Clarke, a former classmate of Edwin Booth, John's older brother. They had nine children. Clarke managed Edwin's theater in Philadelphia.[2] The Walnut Street Theatre was perhaps the most prestigious theater in Philadelphia, opening on February 2, 1809.[3] Edwin Booth purchased the theater in 1863.[4] Also, John Wilkes Booth was a resident of Philadelphia, a fact that came to light when the Civil War draft started, which he managed to successfully dodge.[5]

John Wilkes Booth brought his sisters Asia and Rosalie, his mother Mary Ann, and his younger brother Joseph to Philadelphia in the summer of 1857. They moved into a mansion on the corner of 13th and Callowhill Streets. Booth had taken an acting job at the Arch Street Theatre for $8 a week.[6] This city was where he would hone his craft as an actor, learning voice techniques from his friend John McCullough.[7] He had key roles in such plays as *The Gamester* and *Lucretia Borgia*. Although some early performances were choppy, he was in demand by top managers, and loved by critics and audiences during his time there.[8]

Booth was also in Philadelphia at a key moment in American history. It was December 13, 1860. South Carolina was considering secession and would be the first state to leave the Union one week later on December 20, 1860.[9] There was a rally in front of Independence Hall on December 13. It was billed as a "Grand Union Assembly," but many people blamed the crisis on abolitionists and the Fugitive Slave Act.[10] Booth later wrote, having listened to these speeches, that abolitionists should be "stamped to death" and "hushed forever."[11]

Philadelphia was also a place he could feel at home, ranting to his sister about his hatred for Lincoln. "He is Bonaparte in one great move, that is, by overturning this blind Republic and making himself king," said Booth. "This man's reelection which will follow his success, I tell you it will be a reign. You'll see, you'll see—that reelection means succession."[12]

On January 11, 1865, Booth was in New York City to buy guns and supplies for the Lincoln kidnapping plot. Did he buy the Deringers then? No. He bought two Spencer carbines, two handcuffs, three Bowie knives, caps, six Colt revolvers, belts, and cartridges, but no Deringers.[13] One of the Bowie knives was likely the one he used to stab Henry Rathbone.

We do know some things about where Booth's gun was manufactured. The gun has the inscription "DERINGER PHILADEL"[14] on the right side so we know it was manufactured in Philadelphia by the Deringer Company. The gun was manufactured in the Deringer plant in the 600 block of Tamarind Street, now called North Hope Street.[15] Gun manufacturer Henry Deringer lived around the block at 612 North Front Street.[16]

When Booth left New York City without a Deringer, did he stop in Philadelphia at any time before the assassination? Yes. Only once, and never came back. He arrived in Philadelphia on Friday, February 10, 1865, to spend some time with his sister Asia.[17] We know he spent the weekend in Philadelphia. Booth then went to New York City to visit his brothers Edwin and Junius. On Wednesday, February 15, Junius wrote to Asia that when Booth arrived on Monday, February 13, "he kept them up all night."[18] So Booth likely left Philadelphia on Sunday,

February 12, or more likely Monday, February 13, to depart for New York City. Therefore, I think we can conclude that the last day Booth spent in Philadelphia was probably Sunday, February 12, 1865.

We also know that Booth was planning to say goodbye to his sister that weekend. The point of this visit was to ensure their financial security, and try to explain to his mother why he had decided to assassinate Lincoln. While at Asia's house, Booth attempted to show her how to use the CSS cipher, but she refused. Booth left at Asia's house $4000 in bonds, documents giving his oil business interests to his brothers, a letter to his mother, and a longer undated letter. That letter read in part:

I know how foolish I shall be deemed for undertaking such a step as this, where, on one side, I have many friends and everything to make me happy...to give up all...seems insane; but God is my judge. I love justice more than I do a country that disowns it, more than fame or wealth...

A Confederate doing my duty upon my own responsibility,

J. WILKES BOOTH[19]

In the original draft of the letter, the last line read: "A Confederate, at present doing my duty upon my own responsibility." Booth for some unknown reason crossed out "at present."[20]

Booth was tying up loose ends and saying farewell to his family. He clearly had decided at this point to assassinate Lincoln. Everything was falling into place. Symbolism was important to Booth. Historian Michael Kauffman made these essential observations:

Even the date seemed right. An assassination on April 13 would reemphasize how fate had driven Booth, and how history had guided him. Not only was it the birthday of

Jefferson, but in the ancient Roman calendar it was a day of reckoning—the Ides. The symbolism was not lost on Booth. But in case anyone would miss the point, he would script his own act in conscious imitation of killing Caesar. He would strike down the president in public, preferably in a theater. He would use a Deringer made in a place called Northern Liberties. He would carry a dagger ornately etched with "America, Land of the Free" on its blade. He would commit the act in full view of an audience, with an accompanying message, in Latin, that would explain it all: Thus always to tyrants.[21]

I think Booth wanted to leave Philadelphia with the murder weapon on Sunday, February 12, 1865, because it was Abraham Lincoln's 56th birthday.[22] What better symbolic action than to buy the Deringer on that date, knowing that he would ensure it would be the president's final birthday. He then left town on Sunday, February 12, feeling satisfied that he was leaving Philadelphia on the president's birthday, with the Deringers. This could account for Booth being in such high spirits when he visited his brothers on Monday night, February 13.

Feeling confident that I have the date for the purchase of the weapons, can we find out where in Philadelphia Booth may have purchased the Deringers? The 1865 McElroy's City Directory for Philadelphia on page 860 listed 13 entries under "Guns & Pistols, Importers, and Makers of."[23] A good way to narrow down this list would be to see if any of these businesses were within walking distance of 13th and Callowhill Streets, the home of his sister Asia. After calculating the distances between the Booth home and these locations, I discovered that none are especially near to that spot. If I had to pick the closest, 409 Chestnut Street seems like the easiest route, and most logical choice. Philip Wilson and Company was listed at that location.[24] Booth may have enjoyed the irony that it was behind, and in view of, Independence Hall.[25] Booth was used to walking to Independence Hall, so that would not have been an obstacle. He was there on December 13, 1860, braving the cold during the "Grand Union Assembly" that was mentioned above.

One other possibility I noticed that might have been an option for Booth was a gun dealer at 131 Walnut Street. This location is just three blocks south of Independence Hall.[26] It would have been a little further to walk, but worth the effort. If Booth found out about this gun dealer in the City Directory, or by doing some research, it would have appealed to his sense of humor, irony, and symbolism. The gun dealer at 131 Walnut was Abraham Peterman.[27] What better way to end the president's life than with a gun purchased from a man named Abraham, just down the street from Independence Hall?

I have concluded that John Wilkes Booth likely purchased the Deringers at either 409 Chestnut Street or 131 Walnut Street, Philadelphia. This was sometime on the weekend of February 10 to February 12, 1865. He then left Philadelphia with the Deringers, one of which was used to kill the president. He departed Philadelphia either on February 12 or on the morning of February 13, 1865, for New York City to see his brothers.

I admit that the other 11 gun dealers are possibilities for where the guns were acquired. I loosely ruled them out because they were a little further to walk to from Asia's home, and would not have carried the same symbolic value as the two I listed. I think those two would have appealed to Booth. To be thorough, I have included in the endnotes a list of the other gun dealers.[28] Another burning question we are likely to never know the answer to is: What unsuspecting clerk sold this gun, not knowing how it would change the course of history? The question then remains what the United States would look like if Lincoln was able to live out his second term.

Chapter 4

Lincoln Survives Assassination Attempt— Assassin Booth Held in Custody

There were three chances for Lincoln to avoid assassination on April 14, 1865. The first was if Secret Service Agent John Frederick Parker had stayed at his post. If that had happened, Parker would have entered the box in the lead and introduced Booth. The president would then have stood up, and could have avoided the head shot. Parker also might have seen Booth draw the gun and stopped him. If Booth had entered the box with Parker, Major Rathbone also would have stood up and seen the gun being drawn. If Parker was leading Booth into the box, it would be much more difficult to draw the gun without being noticed in that confined space.

Parker was a curious choice to be guarding the commander-in-chief. He had been in trouble before for drunkenness, sleeping on the job, cursing, and displaying "conduct unbecoming of an officer."[1] Somehow, he managed to avoid punishment and remained on the Metropolitan Police Force. That evening, Parker showed up three hours late at 7 p.m. When the play began, he sat outside the president's box, but grew restless. He decided to leave his post to watch the play from the first gallery. At the intermission he then went for drinks at the Star Saloon, next to Ford's Theatre, staying there the rest of the night.[2]

The second chance for Lincoln to avoid the assassination was if the gun Booth was using had misfired. As I will explore with the Garfield and McKinley assassinations, many guns in the 1800s and early 1900s contained defective ammunition, and misfired. This was a possibility with Booth's single-shot Deringer. Unfortunately, the gun did not misfire—and hit its intended target, the back of the president's head.

The third chance for the assassination to be stopped was if Major Henry Rathbone had stood up when Booth entered, confronted him, and prevented him from drawing the weapon. In fact, Rathbone blamed himself for the rest of his life, thinking he could have stopped the assassination. His wife Clara described how he suffered from "physical ailments, constant fears, and terrible delusions" that got increasingly worse over the years as he descended into madness and depression. Every year on the anniversary of Lincoln's assassination, reporters asked the couple questions, which only increased Rathbone's feelings of guilt. Clara wrote: "In every hotel we're in, as soon as people get wind of our presence, we feel ourselves become objects of morbid scrutiny...Whenever we were in the dining room, we began to feel like zoo animals. Henry... imagines that the whispering is more pointed and malicious than it can possibly be."[3] Perhaps it was inevitable that Henry would shoot his wife to death on December 23, 1883.[4] Immediately after, he tried stabbing himself to death, but survived the wounds. He later died in a German insane asylum, on August 14, 1911.[5] When Lincoln died on April 14, 1865, Clara's fate was sealed as well. If Lincoln had survived the assassination, Henry never would have descended into madness.

What would a second term look like for Abraham Lincoln? He spent his entire time in his presidency trying to preserve the Union as a commander-in-chief. It would be interesting to see if he could have shifted to being a successful peacetime leader. One obvious point to make is that if Lincoln had lived through and completed his second term, the country could have avoided the disastrous presidency of racist southern Tennessee Democrat Andrew Johnson. Johnson did everything he could to stand in the way of legislation passed by the Congress. He vetoed the 1866 Civil Rights Act which stated that "all persons born in the United States" (except for Indigenous groups) were "hereby declared to be citizens of the United States" and that "such citizens of every race and color...shall have the same right...as is enjoyed by white citizens."[6] His veto was overridden by the Congress, but Johnson refused to enforce this law that went into effect on April 9, 1866. This was the one-year anniversary of Lee surrendering to Grant. To placate the racist president, and his expected veto, Congress deleted the following key part of the Act: "There shall be no discrimination in civil rights or immunities among the inhabitants of any State or Territory of the United States on account of race, color, or previous condition of servitude."[7]

If Lincoln had been president, he would have signed this law, not vetoed it, and the provision left out would have been included. Lincoln also would have enforced this law. Another obstacle Johnson placed in the way of former slaves was his effort to destroy the Freedmen's Bureau, established by Congress on March 3, 1865.[8] It provided blacks with housing, food, medical assistance, legal aid, schools, and the chance to regain land lost in the Civil War.[9] In February 1866, Congress passed a bill to reauthorize the Bureau, giving it more aid and more extensive legal authority. Johnson vetoed the bill. A weaker version was then passed that allowed Johnson to remove people from the Bureau and replace them with racist Democrats. He also then began issuing pardons to former Confederates, restored their land and their weapons, and stopped land transfers to blacks.[10] None of this would have been done by Abraham Lincoln. The Freedmen's Bureau was Lincoln's idea, passed in his administration.[11] He would have seen to it that it succeeded, and transformed the lives of former slaves as it was intended.

The Radical Republicans in Congress eventually had enough of Andrew Johnson and decided to impeach him. He had violated the Tenure of Office Act, which stated that the president must get the approval of the Senate to fire members of the cabinet. Johnson fired Lincoln ally and Secretary of War Edwin Stanton without Senate approval. This plus his failure to enforce laws meant to help former slaves were grounds for his impeachment in the House of Representatives. The Senate then conducted a trial, but failed to convict Johnson by one vote.[12] This was a dangerous precedent to set for future presidents. The message was that a president could be as damaging to former slaves as Johnson was, and still remain president. With Lincoln as president in his second term, this trial of course never would have happened. Stanton would have stayed in place as Secretary of War and would have helped Lincoln enforce the Reconstruction Acts, if they needed to be passed.

In fact, the next several years would have been spent implementing Lincoln's vision of the right to vote for educated former slaves and for soldiers who fought in the war. He also wanted to see that the right to vote would be enshrined in each state constitution before states could rejoin the Union. He talked about the "Louisiana Model" in his final address at the White House on April 11, 1865:

> Louisiana [has] sworn allegiance to the Union, assumed to be the rightful political power of the State, held elections, organized a State government, adopted a free-state constitution, giving the benefit of public schools equally to black and white, and empowering the Legislature to confer the elective franchise upon the colored man. Their Legislature has already voted to ratify the constitutional amendment recently passed by Congress, abolishing slavery throughout the nation.[13]

Could you imagine a world where the former Confederate states were forced to ensure equal education of black and white students, and the right to vote for the "colored man"? This would have allowed for a whole generation of students to become civic and political leaders. Many of them would likely have been able to run for sheriff, senator, and governor in these states, working against the prevailing racism, knowing Lincoln had their back. Lincoln would see to it that the Ku Klux Klan (KKK) died in its crib. He would never allow such an organization to exist that would threaten his dream of a "new birth of freedom" that so many had died for in the Civil War. Imagine a world without lynching, rapes, fake elections, burned schools and churches. Imagine the next hundred years with no one living in terror.

Lincoln was insistent about this for other states in that final speech. "What has been said of Louisiana will apply generally to other States...Important principles may, and must, be inflexible." Then Lincoln made it clear to the South that he was ready to bring the hammer down on them if they did not comply, issuing a cryptic warning at the end of his remarks: "It may be my duty to make some new announcement to the people of the South. I am considering, and shall not fail to act, when satisfied that action will be proper." These were his last words ever spoken in public. Ready to act if his nation needed him. The good work not over yet to repair a wounded nation.

After eight years in office there would be calls for Lincoln to run for a third term in 1868. If he had been elected again, he would have turned 60 years old on February 12, 1869, just before inauguration the following month. I think retirement would have been much more appealing to Lincoln and his family. I imagine, with the stress of the Civil War over, his health would have improved in the second term. Spending the waning years of his life with his beloved Mary would have meant more to him than another four years as president.

They would likely have visited Jerusalem after Lincoln left the presidency. Mary Todd Lincoln said that her husband wanted "to visit the Holy Land to walk in the footsteps of his savior." He confided this to her in their last moments in Ford's Theatre.[14] It would be fitting if he had passed away in Jerusalem, likely around 1870 or so, when they finally got around to making the trip.

Either way, the president was looking forward to better times, and enjoying his life for once. The war was over and he was ready to begin a new phase. On a carriage ride on April 14, 1865, before going to Ford's Theatre, Lincoln told Mary: "We must both be more cheerful in the future—between the war and the loss of our darling Willie, we have both been very miserable."[15] Unfortunately, this hope for a better future was ended when John Wilkes Booth unlocked a century of misery for former slaves by firing that bullet into the back of Abraham Lincoln's head.

Part II

The Assassination of President
James Garfield

Chapter 5

Mutual Hatred

By July 1881, many people in the United States wanted to see President James Garfield dead, and just one was his would-be assassin, Charles Guiteau. After a stirring inaugural address, the Civil War veteran was looking to change things. The young president called out the southern states for inaction on voting rights, promising "the new birth of freedom" for former slaves that Lincoln's party had fought and died for. He was making improvements in the corrupt patronage system, and forming enemies with a powerful New York State senator. It had been a busy four months in office for Garfield. He was looking forward to a summer respite to plot his next moves—when fate stepped in. As we will explore later, a friend of his postmaster general seemed to know he was a marked man, with so much change afoot.

To say that New York Senator Roscoe Conkling hated James Garfield with a passion few have seen in American political history might be an understatement. The short but intense narrative of their mutual dislike for one another will lead any casual observer to see why many people logically concluded that Conkling would have liked nothing more than to see President Garfield eliminated.

It is useful to begin this analysis by pointing out that at this point in American history, the Republican Party was deeply divided between two warring factions known as the Stalwarts and the Half-Breeds. The Stalwarts were led by Conkling and were defenders of what was known as the "spoils system," whereby they could control federal and state appointments through nepotism and cronyism. The Half-Breeds, led by Maine Senator James G. Blaine, advocated for reform of this system, seeking to replace it with a civil service system. This system, much like the one in place today, would award government jobs based on merit.[1]

The rift between Conkling and Garfield began at the 1880 Republican National Convention held in Chicago. Conkling was undoubtedly at that time one of the most famous of all United States senators, wielding considerable influence and leadership in the State of New York as head of the Stalwart wing of the Republican Party. As a fellow Stalwart, former President Grant was seeking a third term at Chicago that summer and counting on Conkling to deliver not just the delegates from New York but also the nomination itself. Conkling had staked his entire political career on securing the nomination for Grant, who led on ballot after ballot but could never quite secure the majority needed for nomination. Soon the delegates turned to a compromise candidate, a leader of the anti-Grant forces, a war hero and a member of Congress: General James Garfield. Just listening to Garfield speak made Conkling "seasick,"[2] and when the Civil War hero was finally picked as the party standard bearer, the senior senator from New York stormed out of the convention hall in a fit of rage.

August 6, 1880, turned out to be quite a pivotal day in the relationship between Conkling and Garfield. As a gesture of party harmony, the nominee agreed to travel to New York City to meet with Stalwart leaders in August 1880. Garfield knew he needed New York's electoral votes and the Conkling machine to win the presidency, but privately insisted he was going to be careful about "mortgaging my future freedom."[3] Conspicuously missing from the meeting was Senator Conkling, who preferred instead to send his political cronies to talk to the general. Garfield later wrote in his journal that "the absence of Sen. Conkling gave rise to unpleasant surmises as to his attitude."[4] The Fifth Avenue Hotel was the scene of a meeting between the nominee and four Conkling allies: vice-presidential nominee

Chester Arthur, Wall Street financier Oliver P. Morton, future New York Senator Thomas Platt, and Conkling friend Richard Crowley. According to Platt's account of the meeting, Garfield acknowledged the unmatched power of Conkling's machine in New York and "assured us that the wishes of the element of the party we represented should be paramount with him touching all questions of patronage"[5] in New York federal appointments. This group of four also wanted a key cabinet post for Morton, especially one that handled a good deal of patronage jobs, such as in the Treasury. With these understandings the Stalwart machine would go to work to deliver the state to the Half-Breed Garfield. It is shocking therefore that Garfield would write in his journal on August 9, perhaps under some political delusion, that he was feeling that "no serious mistake has been made and probably much good has been done. No trade, no shackles and as well fitted for defeat or victory."[6] Both sides came away from this meeting with very different interpretations as to what had transpired, and as we will see, it became the source of further tension between the two men.

As the election approached, Conkling made a grudging effort to campaign for the party. However, Garfield could not help but notice the "narrow and unmanly" way in which the New York Senator made "such a manifest effort...to avoid mentioning the head of the ticket" in his speeches. Garfield privately called Conkling a "petulant spoiled child."[7] Yet, in the minds of the Stalwarts, the fact that Garfield carried New York by only 21,000 votes, and with it the presidency, seemed to further indebt him to the Conkling forces in New York.

Tensions grew deeper when the president-elect turned to the fine art of cabinet making. One sign that Conkling would yield little power within the Garfield administration was when the president-elect picked James Blaine as Secretary of State. Blaine was the leader of the Half-Breeds and was intent on exerting enormous influence over Garfield.[8]

The president-elect also felt massive pressure to appoint Morton to the Treasury Department but held steadfast in his refusal. Garfield told Morton himself, "I will not tolerate nor act upon any understanding that anything has been pledged to any party, state or person."[9] Conkling took this as another personal insult, as did Morton. Lucretia Garfield, the president-elect's wife, joined in the fray. She sent a heated letter to her husband on January 21, 1881, that prescribed a radical measure to end this ongoing conflict within the Republican Party. "Mr. [Whitelaw] Reid [editor of *The New York Herald Tribune*] told me this morning that Morton had been very ugly in his talk about you, using the expression that has been so gratifying to the Conkling clique, 'That Ohio man cannot be relied upon to stand by his pledges,'" she wrote after a brief stay at Reid's New York City home. "You will never have anything from those men but their assured contempt, until you fight them dead."[10]

In the end, Conkling got very little from the incoming administration's cabinet. Garfield settled on Thomas James, postmaster of New York, to be the Stalwart representation in the cabinet. James would serve as postmaster general, but this did not please the New York State Senator one iota. James, although a friend of Conkling's, had a fierce independent streak, a reputation for honesty, and a record of clean government, just the type of politician Conkling could not control. The day before the inauguration, Platt, Arthur, and Conkling confronted the president-elect, insisting that they had been cheated, with Conkling becoming verbally abusive toward Garfield, stating that he had broken pledges made in New York City.

After Garfield was sworn in on March 4, 1881, with Conkling standing right behind him, tensions cooled off a bit due to a slew of Stalwart appointments the president made rather swiftly. He sent nine New York State reappointments to the Senate, all men backing Conkling, including US attorneys and postmasters. He even appointed Morton to be the French ambassador, a position

Morton readily agreed to.[11] However, the tenuous goodwill that these appointments may have created was all but destroyed by a political bombshell dropped on the Senate on the afternoon of March 23, 1881, less than three weeks after Garfield took the oath of office. This would be the final straw for Conkling, a clear tipping point for him in his relationship with the new president.

The collector for the Port of New York handled a large portion of revenue in the State of New York, and whoever headed this port authority was sure to be responsible for a wealth of patronage jobs as well. Since the summer of 1878, Conkling ally Edwin Merritt had been collector of the authority, with two years remaining on his contract in 1881. That all changed when the new president sent him to London as general consul and appointed William H. Robertson to replace him that fateful day in March 1881. Robertson was a Half-Breed, and a political rival of Conkling.[12]

Conkling retaliated by releasing an embarrassing campaign letter in which Garfield suggested that all civil servants should donate to political campaigns. The New York Senator also worked behind the scenes to delay all Garfield appointments sent to the Senate, including Robertson. The president then withdrew all his appointments, even the New York ones, except for Robertson.[13] Arthur, Platt, and Conkling sent one last personal appeal to the president to withdraw the appointment, with Arthur even visiting the White House. The vice president said Garfield's actions would surely spell the end of the Republican Party in New York. The president responded that he did not want war, "but if it is brought to my door the bringers will find me at home."[14] Nothing was going to change his mind. Robertson was confirmed by the Senate as the new collector of customs for the Port of New York on May 18, 1881.[15] Conkling's next move shocked his fellow senators and much of the nation. He and New York junior senator, Tom Platt, decided to jointly withdraw their membership in the United States Senate.

Chapter 6

Silencing an Agent of Change

Regarding civil rights, Garfield saw himself as having the moral authority to change things because he was a general and a Civil War hero. He was not just the president, but a real commander-in-chief, like Washington and Jackson before him. His inaugural address contained full statements of resounding support for former slaves:

> The elevation of the negro race from slavery to the full rights of citizenship is the most important political change we have known since the adoption of the Constitution of 1787. No thoughtful man can fail to appreciate its beneficent effect upon our institutions and people. It has freed us from the perpetual danger of war and dissolution. It has added immensely to the moral and industrial forces of our people...The influence of this force will grow greater and bear richer fruit with the coming years.[1]

Garfield was saying that full citizenship for former slaves was the most important thing to happen since the founding of the Republic. The country no longer had to worry about war, and could grow stronger now because former slaves could take part fully in the nation's economy. Without slavery, the nation could finally claim a moral authority to do great things.

Garfield continued:

> No doubt this great change has caused serious disturbance to our Southern communities. This is to be deplored, though it was perhaps unavoidable. But those who resisted the change should remember that under our institutions there was

no middle ground for the negro race between slavery and equal citizenship. There can be no permanent disfranchised peasantry in the United States. The emancipated race has already made remarkable progress. With unquestioning devotion to the Union, with a patience and gentleness not born of fear, they have "followed the light as God gave them to see the light."...They deserve the generous encouragement of all good men. So far as my authority can lawfully extend, they shall enjoy the full and equal protection of the Constitution and the laws.[2]

The president was saying the resistance to equal rights for former slaves in the South was "deplorable." Garfield made it clear that it was within his authority to come down on the South to ensure equal rights for this formerly disenfranchised race. They would not be forgotten in his administration. The president did not stop there. He knew that if these former slaves were to have any hope of a voice during Reconstruction, they needed to be able to vote. The Ku Klux Klan had been stopping this for the past several years through intimidation and violence. Garfield was going to see an end to this in his administration. He continued:

The free enjoyment of equal suffrage is still in question, and a frank statement of the issue may aid its solution. It is alleged that in many communities negro citizens are practically denied the freedom of the ballot. In so far as the truth of this allegation is admitted, it is answered that in many places honest local government is impossible if the mass of uneducated negroes are allowed to vote. These are grave allegations. So far as the latter is true, it is the only palliation that can be offered for opposing the freedom of the ballot. Bad local government is certainly a great evil, which ought to be prevented; but to violate the freedom and sanctities of the suffrage is more than an evil. It is a crime which, if persisted in, will destroy the Government itself...

It should be said with the utmost emphasis that this question of the suffrage will never give repose or safety to the States or to the nation until each, within its own jurisdiction, makes and keeps the ballot free and pure by the strong sanctions of the law. But the danger which arises from ignorance in the voter cannot be denied. It covers a field far wider than that of negro suffrage and the present condition of the race. It is a danger that lurks and hides in the sources and fountains of power in every state. We have no standard by which to measure the disaster that may be brought upon us by ignorance and vice in the citizens when joined to corruption and fraud in the suffrage...[3]

The president also knew that the problem facing former slaves was not just unique to the South. He also called out the northern states to be part of the solution to achieve full equal rights for black people. His solution was a radical idea: safe universal education for the races. If former slaves could read and write, this would truly empower them. He continued:

To the South this question is of supreme importance. But the responsibility for the existence of slavery did not rest upon the South alone. The nation itself is responsible for the extension of the suffrage, and is under special obligations to aid in removing the illiteracy which it has added to the voting population. For the North and South alike there is but one remedy. All the constitutional power of the nation and of the States and all the volunteer forces of the people should be surrendered to meet this danger by the savory influence of universal education...

In this beneficent work sections and races should be forgotten and partisanship should be unknown. Let our people find a new meaning in the divine oracle which declares that "a little child shall lead them," for our own little children will soon control the destinies of the Republic...

They will surely bless their fathers and their fathers' God that the Union was preserved, that slavery was overthrown, and that both races were made equal before the law.[4]

Both races being "equal before the law" was the goal of the next four years. That truly would have been transformative for the broken nation. Charles Guiteau had other plans.

Guiteau had spent most of his life running from creditors, landlords, and getting kicked out of the utopian "free love" commune in Oneida, New York. He stalked President Garfield for weeks before the assassination, having several other chances to kill him, including when the president was walking with his wife after church services. He even gained entry to the White House, seeking employment, but was banned by the guards for his strange behavior. He wrote countless letters asking for appointments and harassing cabinet members, inventing grand stories of his support during the campaign for president. He had visions of grandeur which led him to the idea of assassination. He was severely delusional, and even abusive to his wife, Annie.[5] Here is what is considered the "official" version of the assassination. It is important to know what are the agreed-upon facts so I can add some additional points that are left out by mainstream accounts of the events.

As Garfield's carriage pulled up outside the Baltimore and Potomac, Charles Guiteau paced the waiting room inside...For weeks, the 39-year-old had stalked the president across Washington, patiently waiting for a chance to gun him down...At around 9:20 a.m., Garfield entered the station alongside Secretary Blaine...As the men strode through the waiting room, Guiteau snuck up behind them and drew his pistol...Guiteau fired two shots at the president from point blank range. The first bullet only grazed Garfield's right arm, causing him to bellow "My God! What is this?" The second shot was more accurate, striking Garfield in the lower back and knocking him to the floor.[6]

Guiteau made an attempt to flee the scene, but was immediately stopped by a police officer and a ticket taker. An angry crowd gathered, and calls began to lynch the assassin. However, Guiteau was quickly whisked away to the Metropolitan Police Headquarters under armed guard. After Garfield was shot, ten doctors began to probe his wound, looking for the bullet. They found nothing. Unknown to them the bullet had missed Garfield's vital organs and lodged in his pancreas. This was a survivable injury. The problem was that the well-meaning doctors had introduced infection into the wound. The president continued to bleed and was eventually taken back to the White House. After a summer filled with various failed efforts to save the president's life, Garfield succumbed to the infection from the gunshot wound, and died on September 19, 1881.[7]

Chapter 7

Evidence for a Conspiracy?

The difficulty in examining evidence for a conspiracy in any assassination is being stigmatized as a "conspiracy nut." However, with many assassinations it is an obvious fact that more than one person was involved, including, of course, the Lincoln assassination, and the assassinations of several Roman emperors. It is difficult when going against the official version of events, so I only want to examine evidence of a conspiracy if there is actual evidence, not conjecture. I do not want to risk my reputation as a professor and historian by being seen as someone who peddles wild theories. It would not be fair to myself, or the search for the truth. However, there are some questions about this assassination that I and other historians have pointed out. With that in mind, is there any evidence for a conspiracy in the assassination of President James Garfield?

One of the best pieces of evidence that we have that supports a conspiracy comes from a "friend" of President Garfield and Postmaster General Thomas L. James. This anonymous "friend" was the center of an astounding story about a credible threat to Garfield's life just three days before the assassination on Wednesday, June 29, 1881. This account of a potential conspiracy to kill Garfield was contained in historian Murat Halstead's *Illustrious Life of William McKinley, Our Martyred President* published in 1901. Halstead may have tucked this story away in here because it fit with the theme of presidential assassination conspiracies. Elsewhere in the book he examines evidence of a conspiracy in the McKinley assassination which will inform our discussion of that murder in Part III.

One thing that establishes the credibility of the following story about a potential conspiracy is to examine the author. Who was Murat Halstead? He was one of the most credible, respected, and prodigious authors, journalists, and historians of the late 1800s and early 1900s.

> After graduating from college in 1851, Halstead briefly practiced law. He also provided articles to various newspapers in Cincinnati and wrote several novellas. In 1853, he became a reporter with the *Cincinnati Commercial*, a local newspaper. Within a year, Halstead became a partial owner of the paper. By 1865, he was the editor of the *Commercial*. The *Commercial* later merged with the *Cincinnati Gazette*, the new paper was called the *Cincinnati Commercial Gazette* and Halstead served as its editor.
>
> As editor of these newspapers, Halstead routinely criticized politicians for their corrupt actions...He also strongly supported the Republican Party's platform.[1]

There are at least 30 scholarly books attributed to him that cover topics and biographies such as the war in the Philippines, the Spanish–American War, Admiral Thomas Dewey, Theodore Roosevelt, Queen Victoria, the Boer War, the Russo-Japanese War, Jay Gould, and the Galveston flood, to name just a few.[2] He was one of the most admired journalists and historians of his time. Therefore, given his stellar track record, we can trust his sources and be confident we are dealing with a reputable author. Halstead is reminiscent of *Washington Post* investigative reporter Bob Woodward. Both men were trained as journalists, exposed corruption, and then moved on to write deep-dive investigative books about the prominent figures of their day.

Let us then parse out the story that this trusted historian chronicled. The date was Wednesday, June 29, 1881, late in the evening. Halstead tells us:

[T]he last time President Garfield dined out was with [Navy] Secretary [William H.] Hunt of Louisiana; he drove to the White House between ten and eleven o'clock, with Postmaster General Thomas L. James, who returning to the Arlington Hotel, met a friend and asked him whether he had seen the president. The friend answered no—he had been over to the White House to make a call, but the president was out driving.[3]

Indeed, it can be verified that Garfield was out driving that night. According to White House usher William D. Allen, the president and one of his sons went for a carriage ride that night.[4] So why did James ask this man if he had seen the president? Who was this "friend"?

At this point, James suggests going back to the White House to see if the president has returned. And so, "[t]he call at the Executive Mansion was repeated." Halstead strangely does not tell his readers the identity of this "friend" who went back to the mansion, only that it was a "friend" of the president. Does he do this to shield his identity for the person's safety? This "friend" clearly knew who James was, and the Postmaster General seemed confident that he could send this person back to the White House at around 11 p.m. This person also appears insistent on seeing Garfield. He had tried earlier to see him, but failed. Whatever he wanted to tell Garfield could not wait another day.

Here was the scene that strange night. Garfield was at the White House. He had just been out all evening with Hunt and James, and then he returned to go on a carriage ride with one of his sons. When Garfield got home, it was likely around 11 p.m. The president would have been exhausted, likely having to spend time with his ailing mother who may have been waiting for him to go to bed. Then this "friend" showed up, for the second time. He easily could have turned him away and told him to wait for another day, but the president met with him anyway. The persistence of this friend's need to see the president, and at such a late hour, speaks to the gravity of what he may have been there to tell Garfield. My guess is that he was there to tell him that Garfield was in danger, because when this "friend" emerged from the White House about an hour later, he was clearly shaken. Assassination was on his mind. Somehow, he knew the president's life was in jeopardy, and he wanted to stop it.

Halstead picked up the story:

> As the visitor left, it was nearly the middle of the night, and passing out he saw there on guard a familiar face, and asked the question, "Were you not here on watch in Lincoln's time?"
>
> "Yes," came the reply. "Many a night before he went to bed he would walk over to the War Department to see if anything had come in the way of news from the war, and I often took pains to walk between the old man and the trees—the same trees you see here now—because I had a fear that there might be some ambuscade, and some devil would shoot him. The old man never seemed to think anything about possible murderers being about, but walked right along. Sometimes it was quite dark, and I felt sort of responsible for the old man, and I was quite glad when I got him back and had the door shut on him.[5]

What this friend of Garfield and James said to the guard next was truly chilling. Again, from Halstead's account: "I think it would be well for you to keep a sharp lookout now, for there are queer people about and strange things said—excitements about what the president has done and will or won't do," he said. "It would not be a bad idea to watch carefully now.'[6] The reply was simple and sensible: "These are not war times. Nobody would hurt the president now."[7]

Is it possible to identify who this guard was to give this story more credibility? If we could just find a guard, or an agent of the Secret Service, who served at the White House from Lincoln's time to Garfield's, then this would be the person the warning was given to. According to the White House's history of the Secret Service: "In November 1864, following a request from District of Columbia U.S. Marshal Ward Hill Lamon, who was a close friend of Lincoln and who guarded him whenever possible, four to five men from the D.C. Metropolitan Police were assigned to guard the White House and protect the president."[8]

One of these men appointed by Lamon was White House guard and Secret Service agent Thomas F. Pendel. According to the White House Historical Association, Pendel was at the White House for 36 years. "By the time Chester A. Arthur succeeded James A. Garfield in September 1881, Pendel had experienced the assassinations of both Lincoln and Garfield."[9] This is our man. A guard at the White House, appointed to guard Lincoln, and still on watch before the Garfield assassination. This must have been the man "the friend" was issuing the warning to. It gives even more credence to the story.

Halstead also points out that at that hour Guiteau was in Jackson Square in front of the White House, looking for a chance to shoot Garfield.[10] This was verified by the research of historian James C. Clark as well.[11] This friend seemed to be keenly aware of a plot to kill the president. How did he find out about this? As was the case with Lincoln and Kennedy, multiple groups of people wanted the president dead. What "strange things" had he heard? Who said this? Was it many people, or just one person? It must have been shocking because it caused him to believe the president's life was in jeopardy just three days before the assassination.

In conclusion, we can trust that the above events happened. Halstead would not make up such an important and sensational story. He was a respected journalist and would hardly put his reputation on the line by spinning yarns. The book this account appeared in was about President McKinley, and would have a wide national audience, like all of his previous books. He knew the story was going to be read throughout the country. That might be why he chose to protect the identity of this "friend" who knew the president's life was in danger. Journalists use anonymous sources frequently to protect their safety and to get closer to the truth. If there was a conspiracy to assassinate Garfield, and this person had information about it, his life might have been in danger too. Think of Bob Woodward using his anonymous source "Deep Throat" to expose the Watergate scandal in the *Washington Post* in the 1970s.

The assassination took place at the Baltimore and Potomac Depot on the corner of Pennsylvania and Sixth at the base of Capitol Hill. This railroad station, where people were often maimed and killed, was "a nuisance which ought to have long since been abated," according to Garfield.[12] While in Congress, Garfield even introduced legislation to replace it, but the bill failed to get passed.[13] A special Pullman car had been added for the presidential party to take them to New York City. The president brought with him several members of his cabinet. The first was Secretary of the Navy William H. Hunt. This man was a former Confederate soldier, turned Radical Republican. He supported the Reconstruction Acts, and served as Louisiana's Republican governor in 1873. He was confirmed by the Senate in March 1881.[14] Garfield may have wanted his support and advice for his upcoming address on civil rights. As a trusted member of the military, Hunt may have offered a sense of protection for the president as well. The second member of the cabinet was Treasury Secretary William Windom. This man was a fellow native of Ohio, and an early member of the Republican

Party dating back to his support in the 1850s.[15] The Secretary of the Treasury was also the head of the Secret Service. This had been established by an Act of Congress on July 5, 1865.[16] The third member of the cabinet to accompany the president was Postmaster General Thomas James. It is likely that the mutual friend of Garfield and James would have told James about this potential plot. Is that why James was coming too? It is quite telling that Garfield picked a member of the military, the head of the Secret Service, and the man who probably knew about this potential plot to assassinate Garfield to travel with him. And it does seem that the president knew something was not quite right.

He also brought with him Secretary of State James G. Blaine. The previous time there was a plot to kill a president, with Lincoln, there was an effort to take out the entire line of succession. If Garfield was worried about a plot to kill him, he may have wondered how extensive it was. Who was involved? Who were the targets? If the top parts of the government were taken out, Secretary of State Blaine and Treasury Secretary Windom were the next in line in the cabinet to the presidency. Interestingly, there was a rumor circulating around Washington within minutes of Garfield being shot that Vice President Arthur had also been shot.[17] It is telling that Garfield picked four members of his cabinet for a simple trip to New York City, especially these four. This trip was one thing only: an escape to safety. They were evacuating to be with a trusted friend, Cyrus W. Field. Garfield initially was going to head straight to Massachusetts to give a commencement speech at Williams College and enroll his sons in his alma mater. Field, who had made his fortune inventing transatlantic cable to connect the United States and Europe,[18] was an old friend and fellow graduate of Williams. According to the James Garfield National Historic Site, "after Garfield's death in September 1881, Field helped establish a subscription fund for the Garfield family.

This fund eventually amassed about $360,000...that was turned over to Mrs. Lucretia Garfield for her use. Some of this money was used to construct the...Memorial Library in the Garfield home."[19] The plan was to spend some time on his boat and then head up to the college. This was a safe place. Instead, tragedy struck.

Guiteau arrived at the train station shortly after 8:30 a.m. and was nervously pacing. What he did next needs to be examined in detail. Author James C. Clark uncovered these bizarre series of events, and I was able to examine them further in the Library of Congress. According to Clark:

> Guiteau approached James Denny, the newsstand operator, and asked him to hold two packages and an envelope. In one package was a letter to reporters:
>
> > ...I have just shot the President. His death was a political necessity because he proved a traitor to the men that made him and thereby imperiled the life of the Republic...
>
> In the other package was a copy of his book, *The Truth*, and a letter to the *New York Herald*.[20]

Clark also uncovered something so consequential we need to examine it in detail. According to Clark, "there were two witnesses who raised the possibility that more than one man was involved in the assassination. Denny, the newsstand operator, said he thought the man who handed him the papers was not the same man [Police Officer Patrick] Kearney had in custody. Another witness, Thomas Culton, said he saw two suspicious-looking men in the depot."[21]

Wanting to investigate this further, I visited the Library of Congress where the Garfield assassination casefiles are located. The first one is labeled "James Denny statement, Criminal Case

14056." The other is "Thomas Culton statement, Criminal Case 14056." After extensive digging through the entire Garfield casefile, I was shocked at what I found. The James Denny statement was there, and I read it. Sure enough, it confirmed what Clark had written. We will deal with the implications of this below.

For the Thomas Culton statement, I painstakingly looked through every single file that relates to the Garfield assassination. It was nowhere to be found. I even asked the clerk if I was missing it. He said the statement might have been misplaced in another file. I searched through each file, and I could not find it. I even went back the next day, thinking I might have missed it, or that they had not given me the entire casefiles. However, I still did not find the statement from Thomas Culton.[22] Did someone steal it or destroy it for the purposes of a coverup? Is it just misplaced somewhere?

Let us deal with what these two witnesses said. If Denny insisted that Guiteau was not the same person who gave him the packages, then who did hand them to him? Did someone know Guiteau was going to shoot the president, and give these items to Denny to implicate Guiteau? Did Guiteau have someone he trusted come with him to give the packages to Denny? Was this important to Guiteau so the world would know why he was doing this? Perhaps Guiteau needed someone else to help him go through with it this time, someone to handle the publicity part of the plan. Maybe that was the other suspicious person Culton saw lurking around before the assassination. Did Culton see two suspicious people with Guiteau? What behavior made them suspicious? Did they have weapons? Were they there to make sure Guiteau went through with the plan? Before we get too far down the rabbit hole, we should remember that without reading the Culton statement we really do not know what he meant by "suspicious." Also, it is possible that Denny did not get a good look at Guiteau, and may have been mistaken.

That does seem unlikely, though, because he handed him two packages and talked to him.

In the final analysis, it does seem likely that this deranged office seeker acted alone. There may have been another plot against the president's life that never materialized. Denny may have made a mistake. Yet I am still left to wonder: What is in that missing file from Thomas Culton? Was it so important that it needed to be destroyed? As with many other assassinations, we are left with more questions than answers.

There is one unusual note on the arrest record for Charles Guiteau from the Metropolitan Police, on July 2, 1881, from when he was taken into custody: "Later that morning a witness came in and volunteered evidence placing the alleged assassin at the scene 'whispering' to a possible conspirator, but after the first shot rang out the witness quickly left the depot."[23] Was this the other suspicious-looking character that Culton saw? Was this the person who dropped off Guiteau's papers? Why did he flee so suspiciously?

What we do know is that when James Garfield died on September 19, 1881, after complications from his gunshot wound, a brighter future for the United States died with him. He likely would have been one of the most influential presidents in American history. Let us examine what that stolen future would have looked like.

Chapter 8

Eight Years for President Garfield

Let us speculate on what a full term for Garfield might have entailed. We do know a little about his plans. His political problems were over. With Platt and Conklin out of the way, having resigned from the Senate, Garfield was free to handle patronage, and his nominations cruised through Senate confirmation.[1] He also had designs on spending some time hiking in the New Hampshire mountains, returning to his farm in Mentor, Ohio, and attending the 100th anniversary of the Battle of Yorktown.[2] That would have been on October 19, 1881.[3] After this, most importantly, he was heading to the Deep South. But why and where? General William Tecumseh Sherman had burned Atlanta into submission in November 1864.[4] Seventeen years later, President Garfield was going to return there.

Garfield's Civil War record was exemplary. He organized the 42nd Ohio Volunteer Infantry, and served with distinction at the battles of Shiloh and Corinth, rising to the rank of brigadier general by September 1862. He played a critical role in the Battle of Chickamauga. At a key moment in the battle when it seemed all hope was lost:

> Garfield mounted his horse, Billy…He was one of the few Union generals to return to the battlefield. For the remainder of the day Garfield watched [Union forces] put on a brilliant defense in keeping the larger Confederate force from breaching his lines. Filled with optimism, Garfield telegraphed [General William] Rosecrans, urging him to send troops…for a counterattack. The reinforcements never arrived, only orders to abandon the position by nightfall.

Though Garfield had little to do with the battle, one of his officers would later say that he performed like a true General, giving encouragement to the troops throughout the fight. For his action a promotion to Major General would follow.[5]

It was this battle, in this state, Georgia, which left the greatest impact on him from his entire time in the military. It set him on a path to the presidency. "In the fall of 1863, Garfield left the army and returned to Washington, D.C., where he soon took his place in Congress. He would remain in the House of Representatives for seventeen years, until his 1880 election as the twentieth President of the United States."[6]

Garfield was planning on making a major speech on civil rights in Atlanta, Georgia, in late October 1881. He would expand on his call for voting rights for former slaves, threatening the South with military occupation again if they did not submit. The state meant a lot to him. It was where his life changed forever. He had formed a close friendship with William Tecumseh Sherman during and after the war.[7] It would make sense to have Sherman with him at the speech, the two former generals reminding the South about who had won the war, in the state that had suffered the most. This address on civil rights would have been a turning point in his administration. He would probably declare war on the Ku Klux Klan. It was time to enforce the three Enforcement Acts that Congress had passed to supervise elections and punish those who interfered. It was time to guarantee former slaves the equal rights and voting rights promised in amendments 14 and 15 to the Constitution, the promise called out in his inaugural address.

In this fight Garfield had a key ally in his attorney general, Isaac Wayne MacVeagh. This man was a fellow Republican Civil War veteran, serving in the Pennsylvania Cavalry until 1863, as well as Chairman of the Republican state committee. He was appointed ambassador to the Ottoman Empire, but resigned in disgust after learning about the corruption in the Grant administration.[8] When Garfield appointed MacVeagh in 1881 to be his attorney general he was quickly confirmed by the Senate. This was a man of integrity he could count on. A real reformer who could take on this issue of enforcing equal rights for former slaves. After four years in office the name Isaac Wayne MacVeagh would have been known throughout the country, and hated in the South. He would probably receive death threats or be the target of assassination attempts by the Ku Klux Klan. Keep in mind that the Department of Justice was created to prosecute the KKK. On July 1, 1870, President Ulysses S. Grant officially created the Department of Justice for the protection of black voting rights from the pervasive violence of the KKK.[9] A little more than a decade later, Reconstruction was over, but this was still the Department's mission.

In fact, when Garfield picked his cabinet, it was a message to the South that Reconstruction in his mind was not over. He filled the cabinet with like-minded Radical Republicans who would carry out his agenda of black suffrage and equality. I already pointed out that Secretary of the Navy William H. Hunt, Treasury Secretary William Windom, and Secretary of State James Blaine were all deeply committed to the Radical Republican agenda. For Secretary of War, Garfield selected Robert Todd Lincoln, Abraham Lincoln's son. For the position of Secretary of the Interior, Garfield tapped Samuel Jordan Kirkwood, known as "Iowa's Republican Civil War Governor."[10]

A call for volunteers was made, and the first regiment from Iowa was equipped with money donated by Governor Kirkwood...In 1875, he was reelected to his third term in the governor's office. After serving a little over a year, he resigned from office to take his seat in the U.S. Senate. He served...from March 4, 1877, until March 7, 1881, when he resigned to accept an appointment in President Garfield's cabinet.[11]

MacVeagh, Blaine, James, Windom, Hunt, Kirkwood, and Lincoln all knew what the Civil War had been fought for. They were all committed Radical Republicans who were ready to carry out the president's agenda for the next four years. As a sign of peace with the South, Garfield could have picked Democrats or moderate Republicans for the cabinet. Instead, he picked a cabinet ready to bring the hammer down on the South. These were men like him, men of honor and strength ready to serve their country and bring a new birth of freedom to former slaves. With these picks Garfield wanted to be ready from the start for all departments of the government to be run by men who believed in equality for former slaves. With Garfield as their leader, the next four years would have been truly transformative, and living hell for the former Confederacy. Historian Benjamin Arrington, from the James Garfield National Historic Site, offered this look at what four years of Garfield could have been like:

> Garfield might very easily have chosen to ignore civil rights and race relations in his inaugural address. He was incredibly knowledgeable about fiscal issues; he cared deeply about education; he wanted to reform and modernize the American naval fleet. He had fought in the Civil War, first as a Union general and then as a Congressman, and had slugged it out in the House of Representatives during Reconstruction. Garfield, once describing himself as "cursed" by his ability to see both sides of every issue, had at various times been a Radical Republican, a moderate, and a conservative. But Reconstruction was over, and even many former Radicals believed the federal government had done all it could or should for African Americans. The temptation for Garfield to look only forward, not backward, must have been great.
>
> Instead, Garfield boldly and directly addressed civil rights. "The elevation of the Negro race from slavery to full rights of citizenship," he stated, "is the most important

political change we have known since the adoption of the Constitution of 1787. No thoughtful man can fail to appreciate its beneficent effect upon our institutions and people." Many southern whites surely recoiled at this statement, and Garfield was already creating an uphill battle for himself to win any southern states in his presumed 1884 run for reelection. "There can be no permanent disfranchised peasantry in the United States," he continued. "Freedom can never yield its fullness of blessings so long as the law or its administration places the smallest obstacle in the pathway of any virtuous citizen."

The early Republican philosophies of equality and governmental activism to benefit all Americans resonated with a young Garfield and stayed with him—even to his inauguration as president. So, to those who knew him then or study him now, it is no surprise that Garfield reiterated his own and the government's commitments to civil rights and equality in his inaugural address. Though many in the Republican Party had moved on from the racial issues of the Civil War and Reconstruction eras and were looking for new alliances with financiers and industrialists, James A. Garfield continued to believe that the government had not only the means, but also the responsibility, to promote equality and opportunity for all Americans.

"We stand today upon an eminence which overlooks a hundred years of national life," he told the crowd, "a century crowded with perils, but crowned with the triumphs of liberty and law." And he would, he promised, help liberty and law prevail again during his administration. With such a leader at the nation's helm, the next four (or perhaps even eight) years had the potential to be good ones.[12]

What Garfield was attempting to do was return his young party to its roots. Radical Republicanism, the party of Lincoln, the party that protected former slaves, the party that fought and died for a "new birth of freedom," was ready to be reenergized by former General Garfield. This 49-year-old president certainly had the energy to do it. He was strong enough to carry his mother, Eliza, up and down the White House stairs.[13]

By 1884, when he would run for reelection, Garfield likely would get a second term. Let us look at the election results from 1884, and speculate how it would be different with Garfield on the Republican ticket. The actual results were 219 electoral votes for New York Governor Democrat Grover Cleveland, and 182 electoral votes for James Blaine.[14] If Blaine carried New York, he would have been elected president. But with Garfield controlling the politics, patronage, and wealth in New York City, he would likely have carried that northern state and been reelected. Even if Cleveland carried New York, the popular president could have carried New Jersey, Maryland, Delaware, Connecticut, and Rhode Island. The corrupt and unpopular Blaine could not carry these solid Republican states. Those states would have given Garfield a second term.

Also, there is a good chance that Grover Cleveland would never become the Democratic nominee if Garfield was seeking a second term. After Garfield's death, the Congress passed the Pendleton Civil Service Act in 1883 that awarded federal jobs on the basis of merit.[15] This was in response to the idea that a "deranged office seeker" could be weeded out in the future if government jobs were based on skill. This would never have been passed in a Garfield administration. Garfield thought government service should be brief, stating: "I would say to every young man and woman in the civil service of the Government, hasten by the most steps to get out of these departments into active, independent business life."[16] Samuel J. Kirkwood, for example, eliminated civil service reform within the Department of the Interior.[17] One of the first states to implement civil service reform was New York State. In fact, the lack of civil service reform would likely remain an issue within the government until the 1900s if Garfield was not assassinated. It might have been an issue picked up by the Progressive Era. This from a brief history of civil service reform from Tompkins County, New York:

> It took the assassination of President James A. Garfield in 1881, to create an outrage sufficient to result in the demise of the spoils system in New York State. President Garfield was assassinated by a disgruntled office seeker...Many individuals and reform groups worked diligently for years to remove the enormous power of patronage from the hands of the governor but for the most part, their pleas to Congress fell on deaf ears. The swell of public indignation was so great that in 1882 the various anti-spoils factions coalesced into a genuine reform movement whose voices were so loud and insistent that even the most influential power brokers could not resist their call for an equitable civil service law and bipartisan civil service system. At the federal level, the Pendleton Bill was passed by Congress in the closing days of 1882 and swiftly signed into law by President Chester Arthur on January 16, 1883. This new federal law embodied an entirely new model—the concept of merit and fitness as qualifiers for appointment. New York State wasted no time adopting a civil service law of its own. Within a few months, Assemblyman Theodore Roosevelt routed a bill through the state legislature and Governor Grover Cleveland signed the measure into law on May 4, 1883. This law provided for a New York State Civil Service Commission consisting of three commissioners: two from one party and one from the other. Appointments to the new commission were made by the governor and they wasted no time getting together. The first meeting of the newly formed New York State Civil Service Commission was May 31, 1883.[18]

Civil service reform in New York State was the major issue during the 1884 campaign that allowed Grover Cleveland to secure the Democratic nomination.[19] Without that record of reform, he would have been just another governor. There was also a scandal that broke out during the campaign that Cleveland had fathered a child out of marriage.[20] With all this baggage, and no record of reform, the country would have opted for the safe choice and reelected Garfield.

Garfield's second term could have been even more transformative. He could have continued his effort to eliminate the KKK from existence, perhaps even threatening military reoccupation in the South. He could have expanded his effort to increase funding for public education, leading to an explosion of middle- and high-school graduates. Black and white literacy rates would increase, leading to a decrease in poverty rates. Just as important, he could have transformed the federal court system with four, or eight, years in office, placing fellow Radical Republicans in the courts. President Chester Arthur had 21 federal judges and two judges to the Supreme Court confirmed during his term. All of these posts would have been available for Garfield to fill.[21] These men would have protected the policies of Radical Republicanism. And toward the end of Grover Cleveland's first term, he appointed two judges to the Supreme Court, Melville Fuller and Lucius Cincinnatus, both Democrats.[22] These appointments would have gone to Garfield, not to mention numerous lower court appointments. By the end of his second term, Garfield could have appointed four judges to the Supreme Court. With these Republicans controlling the Court, how would they have ruled on *Plessy v. Ferguson* in 1896, a case that codified the separate but unequal status of Jim Crow America? Would they not allow that to stand? Would America's public schools get integrated in the 1890s, with W.E.B. DuBois leading the integration movement?

The implications are truly earth-shattering if Garfield was true to his word on making sure former slaves lived in a free society. If his Republican Party was going to head in this direction in the 1880s, and into the 1890s, they never would have embraced a man like Ohio Governor William McKinley. He showed zero interest in protecting black people and their rights. For evidence of this, just look at McKinley's reaction to the massacre on November 10, 1898, in Wilmington, North Carolina. Hundreds of black citizens were massacred by members of the KKK after the latter took control of the town's government and newspaper.[23] McKinley's Department of "Justice" did nothing to prosecute anyone involved in this insurrection.

Another possibility regarding McKinley is that he would embrace the reforms of his fellow Republicans and run as a reformer. He was in fact a Civil War veteran like Garfield and Grant. He may have felt that the only way to secure the Republican nomination would be to portray himself as a man of the people, and pledge to continue the policies of integration of Lincoln's Republican Party. Either way, if he never got nominated, or became a man of the people, there would be no McKinley assassination in 1901. Leon Czolgosz would never have bought that gun in 1901 if he thought McKinley was doing what he could to help the common people. The motive to kill him would not exist. Is it too much to suggest that if Garfield had survived, another president would have as well? When Charles Guiteau purchased that gun, and pulled that trigger, he may have sealed McKinley's fate as well.

The twentieth century likely plays out differently as well with eight years of Garfield. If the Republican Party continued to be the party of Lincoln into the 1900s, fighting for former slaves and their children, they might now be the party that African Americans vote for in modern times, not the Democratic Party. Would Franklin Roosevelt and John F. Kennedy have been Republicans? Would the Democratic Party ever have felt the need to change in 1948 if Republicans had never abandoned former slaves? I think we need to reflect for a moment on just how much our country lost when President James Garfield died on September 19, 1881. If he had set his party on the path back to its roots, fighting and dying for former slaves, the suffering of their descendants would not have lasted into the 1900s. When he died that day, so many of the children of the former slaves may have died with him.

Chapter 9

The Second Gun

What gun deprived the United States of this brighter future? In the four cases we are examining, this is the one case where we know for certain that the assassin deliberately selected the weapon with a sense of its historical importance. There are two places that played an important role in the acquisition and purchasing of it. I will examine each individually and see how they both played a key part in the story of how Guiteau was able to purchase the weapon.

Guiteau's gun was a .44-caliber British Bull Dog pistol. It had five chambers, with a two-and-a-half-inch-long barrel. Each chamber was one-and-a-quarter inches long, giving it impressive firing power. In fact, the gun was so powerful it tended to be uneven as it was fired. Also, moisture could reduce its firing power.[1]

Gun historian Kristin Alberts says:

The pocket revolver known primarily as the "British Bull Dog" was first produced by P. Webley & Sons of Birmingham, England, in 1872. Its appeal was so great that the 'British' Bulldog was adopted and copied by gun manufacturers in Belgium, Spain, France, and the U.S. Though American-made Bulldogs came from the armorers Iver Johnson, Harrington & Richardson, Forehand & Wadsworth, and several other makers who quickly went in and out of business, the Webley versions are rightly considered the real McCoy...

[T]he hay day (sic) of the Bulldog was in the 1870s to 1880s, a time when it was known for its affordability and reliability, consequently making it one of the most popular pocket pistols in both Europe and America...The inexpensive, yet solidly made little dogs...were available to everyman...

Bulldogs are quickly recognizable by the bird's head grips, generally made of either walnut or pearl. However, there are many fine examples with sweet ivory grips and delicate engraving. Most had a blued finish, but some nickeled models have survived as well. The revolver is generally dressed with simple fixed sights, a large looping trigger guard, curvaceous hammer spur, and weigh[s] in around 20 ounces.[2]

This was the perfect gun for an assassin. It was cheap, easy to fire, and could be concealed within clothing without anyone noticing. The two locations and key events in how Guiteau acquired the weapon are summarized by historian James C. Clark. There are some things he leaves out, and gets wrong, that we will subsequently deal with.

To raise money [Guiteau] turned to a distant relative, George Maynard...On March 12, Guiteau visited Maynard and asked for money to pay some board bills. He said he expected to receive a check for $150 within a few days. He reappeared at Maynard's office on June 8 and asked for an additional $15. He said he received the check for $150 but needed it to pay his board bills. Another check for $500 was on the way, but he needed the $15 to tide him over until he was named consul to Paris. The money was actually to purchase a pistol. Maynard lent Guiteau the money, and Guiteau went to John N. O'Meara's store at the corner of 15th and F Streets, just a block from the White House. Guiteau had never fired a pistol before and asked O'Meara about the guns. He narrowed his choice to two guns: a pearl-handled pistol, which cost $10, and a pistol with a hard-rubber handle that cost $8. He decided on the more expensive one because it would look better in a museum. O'Meara agreed to sell him the pistol, a small knife, and a box of cartridges for $10. To practice he went down to the banks of the Potomac and shot at branches in the water.[3]

There are several aspects of Clark's reconstruction of events that we can add to, and even correct. The 1881 Boyd's City Directory for the District of Columbia is useful in this respect. The place where Guiteau bought the weapon was "John. U. O'Meara's Sporting Bazar (sic)."[4] Clark got the middle initial wrong. Sporting goods stores were the location where people purchased firearms in the 1800s, early 1900s, and even today. I checked elsewhere in the directory, and "U" is the middle initial five other times when this business appears in other highlighted texts or advertisements. Also, O'Meara paid for these advertisements, so he was unlikely to get his own middle initial wrong. We also know from this advertisement exactly where the store was: "Cor of 15th and F St. Opposing U.S. Treasury." This store was opposite the U.S. Treasury and also the east lawn of the White House. Clark mentioned it was on the corner of 15th and F, but not which corner. Now we know the exact location. It was the northeast corner, where the Washington DC Economic Partnership is as of 2023.[5]

We also know, according to the City Directory, where Guiteau visited Maynard. This information was not mentioned by Clark, but it is essential to the story. Maynard's office was at 1413 G Street NW. This is the location of the American Automobile Association as of 2023. Having walked the area myself, I know that Maynard's office would have been about a four-minute walk around the corner to O'Meara's.[6] The likely sequence of events was that Guiteau got the money from Maynard, walked around the block, and went directly to O'Meara's to purchase the gun. Guiteau may have wanted to use the money immediately before he wasted it on something else. The "Bazar" may have been in view of Maynard's office. The entire time from acquiring the money from Maynard, walking around the block, and purchasing the "Bull Dog" was probably less than an hour. Often when we study assassinations we only focus on the date of the assassination or when the president died. Equally important is the day when the assassin bought the gun and determined to end the president's life. The date was Wednesday, June 8, 1881. Although Garfield did not know it, his fate was already sealed.

Chapter 10

Where Is the Gun That Killed President Garfield?

One of the unanswered questions about the assassination is why Guiteau only fired two shots at the president. The first shot missed him entirely, shattered some glass, and landed in a piece of putty.[1] The second shot hit Garfield in the back, just above the waist, and four inches from the spinal column.[2] It was an injury he might have recovered from if it had not been for several doctors probing his wound with their infected fingers.[3] Despite having a clear view of the president and time to escape, Guiteau stopped firing after two shots, leaving three in the chamber. He could have shot at Simon Camacho, or Police Officer Patrick Kearney, both of whom stopped him on his flight from the station, but he did not.[4]

The lack of other victims, and the focus on the president, led people to forget about the murder weapon. Guiteau was not shooting at other people, so there was no need to get the gun from him. In fact, it was found in his hip pocket when he arrived at the police station. He had the chance to shoot at the guards who took him into custody, but he did not. After the shooting Guiteau was taken to "4th St Pennsylvania Ave NW," the location of the Metropolitan Police Headquarters.[5] This was two blocks away from the corner of Pennsylvania and Sixth, the location of the Baltimore and Potomac Depot where the shooting took place. The gun of course went with Guiteau. At headquarters Chief Detective Joseph Acton thought they were joking about Garfield being shot, but when Guiteau confirmed it, the joking was over. Police Officer Kearney, who had arrested Guiteau, finally realized the president's assassin was standing in police headquarters with a loaded revolver. "Give me that pistol," Kearney said, and Guiteau handed it to him.[6] Up until this moment, from when the gun was purchased until now, it had been in the possession of the assassin. If we are establishing a chain of custody, the first person to take possession of the gun was Patrick Kearney in the DC Metropolitan Police Headquarters. The assassination took place at approximately 9:20 a.m., on July 2, 1881.[7] The assassin probably reached headquarters and handed over the gun by around 10:30 a.m.

What happened next with the gun is shocking, and at the time, no one realized the implications of the tests done on the weapon. We need to make a brief detour into 1880s ammunition, and document how it could be unreliable. This discussion will inform our analysis of the gun used to assassinate President McKinley. A gun is only as good as its ammunition. Many guns in the 1800s and early 1900s misfired due to a short gunpowder load. The bullets would be no more than blanks, sometimes bounce harmlessly off the intended target, or cause the gun to fail and lose its accuracy. This problem persisted into the 1900s. During World War I when machineguns were first mounted on airplanes, their guns would often jam due to defective ammunition. The best pilots inspected their ammunition and discarded the defective bullets before loading the gun to make sure this potentially deadly mishap did not happen in midflight.

The next person to take possession of the gun was Metropolitan Police Detective George W. McElfresh.[8] McElfresh had occupied another role in a different assassination. According to historian James O. Hall:

> in the fall of 1864 it was decided that a detail of the Washington Metropolitan Police force would be assigned to protect the President. This was at the request of Ward Hill Lamon, United States Marshall for the District of Columbia and a close friend of Lincoln's. Lamon had become increasingly fearful

for the President's life. On November 3, 1864, the initial detail was composed of John R. Cronin, Alphonso Dunn (or Donn), Thomas F. Pendel, and Alexander (or Andrew) C. Smith. Changes were occasionally made, although the detail was never more than 5 officers at any one time. Other officers who served in the detail included William S. Lewis, William H. Crook, George W. McElfresh, Thomas T. Hurdle, Joseph Shelton, John F. Parker, and D. Hopkins.[9]

Parker, not McElfresh, was on duty the night of the Lincoln assassination. Perhaps McElfresh felt some remorse that another assassination had happened on his watch. McElfresh asked two members of the Army to test the gun's firing power. He knew this information would be important in an upcoming trial to convict Guiteau quickly. The names of the Army men as reported in the *Washington Post* on July 10, 1881, were "O. M. Poe and Jas M. Whittemore." McElfresh had requested, and was granted, an order to test Guiteau's gun and its ammunition by United States District Judge G. B. Corkhill.

The Army personnel subsequently stated: "We have to report that in compliance with your request we have examined and fired the pistol put into our hands by Detective G. W. McElfresh." McElfresh had removed the three unused bullets, and given the Army three more for comparison, for a total of six. The Army saved one for "weighing" comparison. This was the only usable one from the three because in testing the others "they failed to explode."[10] Is that why Guiteau stopped firing? Did his gun jam after the second shot? Did he inspect, or weigh, the bullets ahead of time to see which were the best ones with the highest gunpowder load? Was the first bullet defective, which would explain how it missed the president? And most compelling to consider: What if Guiteau had loaded the defective bullets first? The gun would have misfired, and Garfield's life would have been spared. If Guiteau had loaded his gun in a different order it is likely the assassination would never have happened. This gun, and the way it was loaded, changed the course of history forever.

After testing, the gun was returned to the Metropolitan Police. It was kept there until it was brought into evidence at the trial of the assassin. The trial took place at the DC City Courthouse, 430 E Street NW, originally built in 1820 as the first City Hall.[11] The trial began on November 14, 1881,[12] and ended on January 26, 1881.[13] The jury deliberated for less than an hour and found Guiteau guilty. He was executed on June 30, 1882.[14] After the trial, the gun was taken from evidence and returned to the Metropolitan Police.

After this it is difficult to determine where the gun went. We do know that it was possibly given to the Smithsonian Division of Armed Forces History and was photographed by them sometime in the late 1800s or early 1900s.[15] If I had to guess, I would think that the gun would have stayed with McElfresh. He seemed the most affected by the assassination, asking for the testing to be done. He likely kept it in his office safe, or perhaps at home. He probably had no desire for it to be displayed in a museum as the assassin wanted.[16] McElfresh died on March 21, 1901.[17] Is it possible that at this point the Metropolitan Police decided to get rid of the gun and donate it to the Smithsonian?

A search of all records in the Library of Congress, the National Archives, and the Smithsonian Institution yields no clues as to the whereabouts of the gun, if it was acquired, or when it was photographed. I contacted the curators and archivists at the Smithsonian in the Division of Political and Military History, the Archives Center, and the Division of Armed Forces History. I asked if they could provide information about when the Smithsonian acquired the gun used to assassinate President Garfield, when it was lost, and when it was photographed by the Division of Armed Forces History. To date (July 2023) I have not received a single reply to any of my inquiries.

It does seem unusual that there is no information about where this gun is today. How could such an important piece of history just get "lost" by our most respected keeper of the nation's historical artifacts, especially a gun used to assassinate a president? Was the gun deliberately destroyed so that the assassin's wish for it to be in a museum could never be granted? That may be the reason. If that is the reason, why hide it? The public would likely support such a decision to never give Guiteau his dying wish. It would seem appropriate to melt it and move on.

Is it also possible that the Smithsonian Division of Armed Forces History only photographed the gun and never acquired it? Is the gun still in the possession of the DC Metropolitan Police? Evidence records from the 1800s do not exist, only arrest records in the National Archives.[18] Does one of the families of the detectives involved, such as Kearney or McElfresh, have the gun in a family safe? Does some morbid collector have the gun? After the assassination there was an effort to collect curiosities regarding Guiteau, including a jar filled with the remains of his diseased brain. This can be viewed at the Mütter Museum in Philadelphia.[19] Was the same effort made to acquire his gun?

Also, where are the three bullets that Guiteau never fired? They were returned to McElfresh after the testing by the Army.[20] How long did they stay in his possession, or in evidence at the Metropolitan Police Department? As I mentioned in regard to the gun, only arrest records from the Metropolitan Police exist from the 1800s in the National Archives, not evidence records. If the gun was handed over to the Smithsonian, were the three bullets handed over as well?

I have a theory. I find it difficult to believe that our foremost keeper of the nation's historical artifacts could ever lose such an important piece of history. I do not think they ever acquired it at all. What I suspect happened was that McElfresh, and possibly Kearney, decided to let the Smithsonian photograph the gun for historical purposes. Then they let some time pass for the story to get out that the gun was "lost." Perhaps there was an assumption that because the Smithsonian photographed it, they also took possession of it, but in reality the Smithsonian never did. In the meantime, the police officers took it upon themselves to destroy it, and the bullets. They were probably feeling guilty about another assassination having happened on their watch in less than 20 years. They wanted no public viewing of this gun or the bullets to make Guiteau into a celebrity or a martyr. He and his gun fit for a museum would be erased from history, never to be on display, liquidated like the assassin himself.

Think, for comparison, of the burning of Adolf Hitler's body by the Russians at the end of World War II, or the sea burial for Osama Bin Laden by American special forces. There would be no shrines for these evil men and their followers. In the situation with Garfield, the detectives would not let the assassin have the final say. The gun and the bullets would have been a permanent reminder of the tragedy. They did not need to be preserved. I have concluded that the reason no one, including the Smithsonian, has come forward with this gun, or the bullets, is simple. The gun and the bullets do not exist anymore. This is for the best. The enduring memory of this assassination should not be centered on some crazed office seeker, or his gun, but instead on President James Garfield, who was truly a great American hero.

Part III

The Assassination of
President William McKinley

This part of the book is personally relevant to this author for three reasons. First, having been born and raised in Buffalo, New York, I know that the assassination of President William McKinley has hung over our beloved city for well over a hundred years now. We feel it as a community that we let this tragedy happen on our watch, in the City of Good Neighbors. It has been our curse to never forget what happened on that horrible September day in 1901. How could we forget when the center of our city bears a permanent reminder of the assassination? In the middle of Niagara Square is the McKinley Monument obelisk, dedicated in 1907, to honor the memory of the dead president.[1]

Second, I feel proud of the research and scholarship I brought forth in my local bestseller *The Secret Plot to Kill McKinley* (Western New York Wares, 2011). In this book, I put forward credible evidence of a conspiracy to assassinate McKinley. Since the publication of the book more than ten years ago, new information has come to light that I wish to share with readers. It has cast a new light on what dark forces may have been aligning against McKinley on that fateful day.

Third, I would like to thank my parents and late grandparents, who started all this passion for me when I was much younger. To say I became obsessed with the McKinley assassination and the Pan-American Exposition is an understatement. They took me to the old Exposition grounds and allowed me to photograph (and pay for developing) endless numbers of pictures so I could find out where the old buildings on the Exposition grounds once stood. Many times, we went to the site where McKinley was shot and where he died. We visited Goat Island to retrace McKinley's trip to Niagara Falls, and Cayuga Island where he broke ground for the Exposition. We took tours of the Theodore Roosevelt Inaugural National Historic Site, where my grandparents had held their wedding reception in the 1940s. I owe a debt of gratitude to them for their patience and for feeding my love of Buffalo, and its history, which still endures.

Chapter 11

The Mystery Man and the Missing Photographer

The basic facts of the McKinley assassination are as follows: President William McKinley was visiting Buffalo, New York, to attend the Pan-American Exposition. This was a world's fair held in Buffalo from May 1 to November 1, 1901. It was meant to celebrate the peace achieved in the Americas after the US victory in the Spanish–American War in 1898, which McKinley had presided over.[1] The president arrived in Buffalo on September 4, and spent September 5 and 6 touring the Exposition grounds and visiting Niagara Falls. The culmination of the trip was a widely advertised meet-and-greet with the public in the ornate Temple of Music on the Exposition grounds. This was scheduled for 4 p.m. on September 6. At 4:07 p.m., Leon Czolgosz fired two shots into the president's chest. The first bullet was short of its gunpowder load and failed to penetrate McKinley, landing harmlessly in his suit. The second shot ended up being fatal, ripping a hole in his pancreas and liver. The assassin's gun had been concealed with a white handkerchief. The president eventually died from his wound on September 14, 1901, in the home of Exposition president John Milburn, on the northwest corner of West Ferry Street and Delaware Avenue.[2]

There is more that we can add to this story that supports evidence of more than one person involved with the assassination. One way is to follow the money trail, a source of income for the assassin that could not have reasonably come from him. Czolgosz's movements are hard to track throughout 1901. His family said that he disappeared for months at a time. Dr Vernon Briggs was tasked with seeking to investigate the assassin's mental state for a potential insanity defense (that went nowhere). Briggs found out that Czolgosz made four trips to Cleveland to visit with Emil Schilling, a member of an anarchist group known as the Liberty Club. Schilling corresponded with Abraham Isaak, a close associate and lover of Emma Goldman, the most prominent anarchist in US history. As treasurer of the Liberty Club, Schilling could have been a source of income for Czolgosz, who had left his family's farm in Warrensville, Ohio, with only $70 in May 1901.[3]

Schilling and Czolgosz first met on May 19, 1901. The two men talked anarchist theory, had dinner, and parted with Schilling giving his new acquaintance some anarchist books to take with him.[4] They met a second time three weeks later, again a week after that, and finally again in August. Czolgosz might have alluded to his plans to kill McKinley, having met with this man several times. In fact, Schilling even asked Isaak to print a warning about him in Isaak's magazine *Free Society*, which appeared days before the assassination. What would provoke Schilling to warn other anarchists about Czolgosz? The warning even admits that Czolgosz had "solicited aid for acts of contemplated violence."[5] Was this to clear Schilling's name, and Isaak's, once the shooting happened, knowing that the plot was already in place? Also, if it was known that this man was willing to commit violence to end McKinley's life, other groups could use Czolgosz as a hired gun.

McKinley was originally scheduled to visit Buffalo on June 13, but his wife Ida took ill in San Francisco in June 1901.[6] President's Day was rescheduled for September 5. Shortly after the original date was canceled, the assassin made his first appearance in western New York where he took a room on the Kazmarek farm in West Seneca. This town is next to Buffalo's southern border. In August 1901, Czolgosz ran out of money. We know this because he could not pay his $1.75 room and board, and he was not employed. Czolgosz told the proprietor Antoni Kazmarek that it was "too hot to work."[7]

At this point something crucial happened in the narrative. The assassin boarded a ship for Cleveland and spent August 29 and August 30 in Ohio.[8] He returned to Buffalo loaded with cash. When Czolgosz arrived at a Broadway Avenue rooming house/tavern on August 31 to ask for a room, he paid his $2 rooming fee in advance. He impressed owner John Nowak by promptly paying his bills throughout his stay and ordered the most expensive drinks at the bar. This "fair sort of man," as Nowak called him, even flashed a roll of bills to John Romantowski, an employee who lived on nearby Sycamore Street. The would-be assassin pulled a $50 bill from the stack just to show Romantowski how much money he had on him.[9]

More evidence of the amount of currency that the would-be assassin was carrying came from the amount he spent to buy the murder weapon. On September 3, Czolgosz bought one of the most expensive, high-quality handguns available in 1901. It was a .32-caliber Iver Johnson revolver. This was the kind of weapon an anarchist had used to assassinate Italy's King Umberto the First, just a year earlier. The gun sold for $4.50 at the Walbridge Hardware Store. Adjusted for inflation that is about $100 or so in 2023, not including the .32-caliber Smith and Wesson cartridges Czolgosz purchased as well for ammunition.[10] This was certainly an upgrade from the defective gun Czolgosz had brought with him earlier in the summer that he used as partial payment for room and board at the Kazmarek farm.[11]

Who gave him all this money? Given the above conclusion that Schilling must have known of Czolgosz's intent to kill the president, or at least commit "acts of violence," if he gave him this money, he can be named as a co-conspirator. If it was not Schilling, the source of this large amount of money that the assassin produced in Buffalo still raises many suspicions.

Who could give Czolgosz that much money so quickly? It could not be from his family, who had not seen or heard from him since July when they received a cryptic letter from him postmarked Fort Wayne, Indiana, saying "it is hard for me to tell you where I'll be."[12] His drifter lifestyle in 1901 would have made it difficult to establish trusting relationships that might quickly produce gifts of large sums of cash. If, however, he was contracted to commit the crime, as part of a wider conspiracy, McKinley's killer would have been provided with enough payment to get the job done.

An additional point to make here is that no one really knows who Czolgosz met with. It could have been anyone, and he may have traveled outside Cleveland. These are just educated guesses put forward by Vernon Briggs. Most of the assassin's time in Ohio in those missing days is unaccounted for. All we know for sure is he left Buffalo in virtual poverty and returned a rich man in just over 48 hours.

The next area of evidence was what happened at the crime scene when a mystery man in line did everything he could to make the assassination of William McKinley possible. He was an essential part of the plot, and I have since come to know his identity. First, though, we need to understand a little more about his actions on the day of the assassination, September 6, 1901.

We need to examine in detail the unusual actions of an anonymous figure who played an essential role in the successful execution of the plot to kill McKinley. He was the man standing directly in front of Czolgosz in the receiving line. He was the last person to shake hands with McKinley before the president was shot. His behavior was truly bizarre, and he correctly caught the attention of the Secret Service, which was the entire point of his presence.

The mystery man did two extremely important things, which I will examine in detail. Both were crucial to allow Czolgosz to blast two rounds into McKinley's chest. First, while moving forward in line, this anonymous man left virtually no space between himself and Czolgosz. Witnesses noticed that he was also leaning backward while walking forward.[13] These two actions allowed Czolgosz to conceal his gun that he was waiting to fire underneath a white cloth. Without this man walking so tightly with the assassin, and then leaning backward to shield the weapon, the Secret Service, or others in line, could have seen the revolver. It would be hopeless to try to shoot the president without a human shield in front, when a gun could be so plainly observed by anyone. Secret Service Agent George K. Foster was asked about this during the assassin's trial:

"Were you observing the people in the line to see if they were armed?" asked Judge Robert C. Titus.

"I was trying to," answered Agent Foster.

"Didn't you see this man with his arm across his breast?"

"No, they were passing too close together."

"The line passed right in front of you, and this man had his arm up with a white handkerchief wound round his hand, and yet you did not see it?"

"No, I didn't see it. And I was looking," said Foster.[14]

The second duty that this strange man performed was also essential to the success of the plot. This anonymous co-conspirator greeted McKinley, firmly grasped his hand, and refused to release it for several seconds.[15] The Secret Service immediately seized him and moved him away from the president, leaving the chief executive unguarded for the next person in line, who was the assassin. With McKinley then unguarded, Czolgosz stepped forward with a clear path to launch two shots into the president's abdomen. On September 7, the day after the shooting, Secret Service Agent Samuel Ireland released a statement to the press that addressed this point.

"I watched [Czolgosz] closely but was interrupted by the man in front of him, who held on to the president's hand an unusually long time. This man appeared to be an Italian, and wore a short, heavy, black mustache," Ireland said. "He was persistent, and it was necessary for me to push him along so that the others could reach the president." The plot seems to count on this misdirection working, and it could not have fooled the agents any better. "I believe that the man ahead of Czolgosz was an associate or friend of the assassin and was there to make way for him to keep his ruse from being discovered until it was too late," said Ireland.[16]

Put together, the combined actions of the "Italian" have all the appearances of premeditated murder. Historian Murat Halstead came to this conclusion as well. "The tragedy was not only planned but rehearsed," he concluded, "an accomplice being ahead of the anarchist…[Czolgosz] knew where the handshaking would take place…and he was preceded by a dummy to clear the way for bloody murder, and the president was in a trap to be slaughtered."[17]

Another question that remains to be answered about the "Italian" is: Where did he go after the shooting? Foster even said that his "general appearance" aroused his suspicions. Why was he not detained, or hunted down? In fact, if this man was not involved, why did he never come forward to clear his name? Any normal person would stay to help the ailing president, especially since he would have seen everything that happened. Instead, he was nowhere to be found. I think this points to his guilt. One reason we know so little about the man is that in the chaos that followed during the moments after the shooting, a mistake was made. The crime scene was cleared.

Marshall of the Exposition Louis L. Babcock made that decision. "Just as soon as the prisoner was down on the ground," he testified at the assassin's trial, "I ran towards the east and motioned to the guards and cried: 'Everybody out!' And the guards immediately cleared the Temple of Music toward the east."[18] Several uniformed military personnel on hand even fixed their bayonets to sweep the masses from the building.

Although this did restore order, many of the witnesses to the murder, and any potential accomplices, were forced out of the building. This provided a getaway for the mysterious "Italian" who had helped hide the assassin's gun and cleared the way of Secret Service protection. In fact, after the shooting, McKinley's bodyguards were more interested in pummeling Czolgosz than tracking down the immediate whereabouts of the man who had just minutes before aroused intense suspicions. He was completely forgotten about in the melee and allowed to melt into the chaos. "The Italian" was probably forced out of the building by some unknowing police officer or soldier, after which he may have just drifted among the mourners until an inconspicuous time arrived that allowed him to pass through the exit gates and disappear into history.

Is it possible to know what this man looked like or who he was? Perhaps the most detailed description ever given of "the Italian" was by a reporter for the *Buffalo Morning Review*, John D. Wells. He was standing near the president, watching the receiving line, and making notes. Wells focused on this man "of unusual aspect—short, heavy, and dark with a heavy black mustache. Under his black brows gleamed a pair of black glistening Italian eyes."[19] On September 7, Secret Service Agent Samuel Ireland described the man in the same way to a group of reporters. "The man appeared to be an Italian and wore a short, heavy, black mustache."[20]

There is more that can be learned about this. In November 2013, I was at a local author book signing at the Buffalo History Museum. I was signing copies of my new book about the McKinley assassination. Ironically this was the former New York State Building, built for the Pan-American Exposition. It remains one of only three remaining buildings from the Exposition. The other two are the Albright Knox Art Gallery (partially open during the Exposition) and the Indian Stockade. McKinley had lunch in the New York State Building the day before the assassination. The president himself may have even felt some apprehension, evidenced by a curious remark he gave to a waiter, Harry Winer, during a luncheon on September 5. Winer had been chosen to wait on the president because he had served McKinley during the 1896 Republican National Convention in St Louis. Perhaps this familiarity was why the president asked Winer, while he was dining in the main court area inside the building, "What's on the other side of that door, my boy?" The waiter replied that it was only gardens and a pool, but the president still did not want him to open it on that hot summer day. Winer got the impression that McKinley may have had a vague sense of fear, only one day before he was shot.[21]

It was in this very room that a man approached me at the author table. He had a curious smile on his face. He said that he had read my book and was very impressed, particularly with the section about the mysterious man in front of the assassin. He then said something quite shocking.

"I know who the man in front of Czolgosz was," he said. "He was my great-grandfather. And yes, he was Italian." I was stunned. I asked him more about this. He replied that it was a well-kept family secret, but since the book came out, he felt like he wanted to come forward with the information. The family had to keep quiet about it. He admitted that he feels his great-grandfather was potentially a part of the plot. He told me his great-grandfather was a ward boss in the Republican Party in Buffalo, and he later confirmed this with me after talking to more members of his family. The implications of this are enormous. Was the Republican Party part of the plot here? Was this a plot to install former New York Governor Theodore Roosevelt, devised by his powerful allies in Buffalo who had helped elect him governor? It seems too sensational. Did they use the anarchists as hired assassins?

The only way that this could make sense is if I could tie it into something else that might provide proof that someone powerful was pulling the strings here. This brings us to the case of the missing photographer. There have been several books written about the McKinley assassination, and I am particularly proud of the fact that I examined how there were no photographs taken of the assassination. No other historian has pointed this out or examined it. No one questioned why. If we probe into this question, we are left with some very difficult conclusions to make. One might reasonably conclude that such a public event would yield photographic evidence, given the fact that many fairgoers brought cameras with them. Yet there are no photos of McKinley inside the Temple of Music, where the assassination took place.

Several photographs were taken of the president throughout his visit. One photo of a smiling President McKinley greeting people and looking at the camera has often been labeled as showing him inside the Temple of Music. However, this photo was taken at a luncheon earlier in the day on the Exposition grounds.[22] The interior of the building is not the spacious and ornate Temple of Music. The last known photograph of McKinley was taken by photographer Jimmy Hare as the president was walking up the steps of the Temple of Music.[23] After that point there is no photographic record of what happened during the assassination. The question needed to be asked: Why?

To provide an answer we need to examine the life of Charles Dudley Arnold. He was the official photographer of the Pan-American Exposition. Arnold was born in Port Stanley, Ontario, on March 19, 1844. He moved to Buffalo by the age of 20. When he was named official photographer of the Pan-American Exposition, he had already accumulated 20 years as a professional photographer. He was also the official photographer for the Columbian Exposition in Chicago in 1893.[24] Arnold's photographs from the Pan-American Exposition have been highly regarded for their crisp, expansive feel. He left nothing undocumented, from the construction of the buildings to their eventual demolition. He photographed people, events, and buildings, outside, inside, and all around Buffalo's "Rainbow City."

The last photograph that Arnold took of McKinley showed the president sitting in a carriage with Exposition president John Milburn and McKinley's private secretary George Cortelyou. The Temple of Music is clearly seen in the background, just next to the carriage. McKinley tipped his hat, smiled, and looked directly into the camera. Arnold had been following the president around for two days, so the photographer was a familiar, friendly face to the president. It was just before 4 p.m. when they arrived. The president would be shot in less than ten minutes. This places Arnold at the scene. He then disappeared. When the shooting was over, Arnold had to be sent for and found to photograph the crime scene. Why did Arnold not go inside? It was strange, out of character, and unprofessional. He had photographed all aspects of the Exposition, including many photographs of the president. This public reception was a highly touted event inside the most beautiful building on the grounds. It would have provided the most magnificent photographs of the president greeting his constituents. This was the money shot, yet he was not there. Why? The question burns and haunts. If he had photographed the line of people, we might have the identity of "the Italian" in front of Czolgosz.

Did someone prevent Arnold from entering the Temple of Music? Was he officially detained, and so prevented from going inside? In all the studies of the assassination, no researcher has addressed this point to provide an answer. If Arnold was deliberately prevented from entering, this might indicate that someone had prior knowledge of the assassination and did not want him to photograph what was about to happen. But who could do this? Arnold's official status allowed him to go anywhere. For him to be denied entry it would have to be someone who had authority, which could place the conspiracy outside the ring of anarchists. For Arnold not to be there at the highlight of the entire Exposition does not make any sense. Logic dictates that his presence would be required to chronicle the only public event that the president had in his schedule.

Jimmy Hare, who took the last photograph of McKinley, also chose not to head indoors. He said in his personal memoir that he had heard McKinley give speeches before so he did not need to go in.[25] That is a strange comment to make since McKinley was not scheduled to give a speech, only shake hands. For some unknown reason both Hare and Arnold instead chose to stay outside in the 82-degree heat (28°C).[26] One must question what larger machinations might have been at work to secretly prevent these men from being where they rightly and logically should have been — inside the Temple of Music taking photos.

Let us combine this newly acquired information with what we already know about Arnold and Hare. It seems that someone in authority had to deny them entry for both not to take photographs. The reason would be to hide the identity of the Italian, who we now know was a prominent member of the local Republican Party. Also, if Arnold was taking photographs, he likely had a good chance to stop the assassination. He could have spotted the gun, or the Italian's strange behavior, and realized something was not quite right. He would probably photograph everyone in line as they entered, and might have noticed the assassin. A full seven minutes went by during which he could have spotted Czolgosz. Arnold likely would have been walking up and down the row of greeters, taking pictures. This would have made the Italian uncomfortable, disrupting his efforts to shield the gun. If he had been there, perhaps Arnold could have prevented the assassination.

One other possibility that I failed to mention at the time of my first McKinley book is something more sinister. Is it possible that Arnold did follow McKinley into the Temple of Music, and took pictures of the assassination, but they were destroyed to cover up the truth of what happened? Is it possible the Republicans used Czolgosz as a patsy? Were they behind the massive influx of cash he got in late August 1901? We really do not know if Czolgosz got that money from Schilling. It is just an educated guess. It could have come from anyone. Did someone in Ohio, McKinley's home state, want to see him eliminated? I am still left to wonder: Why are there no photographs of the assassination of William McKinley? Logic dictates that there should have been. Until I get a good answer, I cannot really say for sure what happened on that tragic day, only that our country, and city, was never the same. Let us examine a world where President McKinley survived.

Chapter 12

McKinley Survives Assassination Attempt

McKinley's life could have been saved, but many mistakes were made. If the Secret Service had stayed in position, and not fallen for the ruse by the Italian, they might have stopped the second, fatal shot from entering McKinley's body. The first shot was a harmless dud, like other bullets left in the chamber. Also, if Arnold had been allowed to photograph all the people in line, this might have made the conspirators abort the mission, or Arnold could have spotted the gun when taking photographs. At the very least, a photograph might have caught the identity of the Italian.

Mistakes were also made with the surgery. McKinley was operated on by gynecologist Matthew Mann, using a mirror to reflect sunlight onto the wound. The operation took place in the ill-equipped Exposition Hospital, with no X-ray machines. Also, the medical director of the Pan-American Exposition, Dr Roswell Park, should have been there like all the other directors, but instead he chose to perform an elective surgery that day in Niagara Falls. He likely could have saved the president's life if he had performed the surgery with proper equipment.[1]

How does the course of history change if President McKinley lives through his second term? I think it largely depends on what happens with Theodore Roosevelt, his vice president. One rumor to dispel was the idea that McKinley would run for a third term. He put an end to this speculation immediately in the second week of June 1901:

> I regret that the suggestion of a third term has been made. I doubt whether I am called upon to give it notice. But there are now questions of the gravest importance before the

administration and the country, and their just considerations should not be prejudiced in the public mind by even the suspicion of the thought of a third term. In view, therefore, of the reiteration of the suggestion of it, I will say now, once and for all, expressing a long-settled conviction, that I not only am not and will not be a candidate for a third term, but would not accept a nomination for it if it were tendered me. My only ambition is to serve through my second term to the acceptance of my countrymen, whose generous confidence I so deeply appreciate, and then with them do my duty in the ranks of private citizenship.[2]

One factor in his decision to want to return to "private citizenship" was the deteriorating health of his wife, Ida. During a tour of the Pacific Coast in the second week of May 1901, the first lady fell gravely ill. The citizens of San Francisco watched and prayed as she hovered near death, but finally recovered.[3] The presidential party returned to Washington DC in June, likely prompting McKinley to issue his statement declining a potential third term. Ida McKinley died on May 26, 1907, at the age of 59, six years after McKinley's assassination.[4] One thing that would have been a consistent feature of McKinley's second term was the distraction of dealing with his wife's health problems. The stress of being first lady would have gotten worse as the years wore on, likely leading to more episodes like the one in San Francisco. By March 5, 1905, when McKinley would have had his first full day as a private citizen, there was a good chance he would be returning to Ohio without his beloved Ida.

Regarding the president's policies, he would have continued his strike-breaking, pro-gold, pro-tariff policies that got him elected with the help of Rockefeller, Carnegie, and Morgan. The Progressive Era reforms of the early 1900s would have been delayed with him in office. I can also see McKinley continuing to look for chances to expand the American empire, putting naval bases in Central and South America to enforce the Monroe Doctrine and to expand democracy. There also would have been more troops deployed, and an effort to bring democracy to Cuba, leading to more American investments there. In fact, in McKinley's second inaugural address he said the most important issue the US was facing was Cuba:

> We face at this moment a most important question, that of the future relations of the United States and Cuba. With our near neighbors we must remain close friends...Ever since the evacuation of the island by the army of Spain, the Executive, with all practicable speed, has been assisting its people in the successive steps necessary to the establishment of a free and independent government...The principles which led to our intervention require that the fundamental law upon which the new government rests should be adapted to secure a government capable of performing the duties and discharging the functions of a separate nation, of observing its international obligations of protecting life and property, ensuring order, safety, and liberty, and conforming to the established and historical policy of the United States in its relation to Cuba.[5]

If McKinley had been able to help Cuba flourish into a functioning democracy, with a free, independent government that ensured safety and liberty, then I suspect the name Fidel Castro would never have been known to history. The Cuban Missile Crisis and the Bay of Pigs Invasion would never have happened.

By 1904, the Republicans would be wise to nominate their popular vice president, former governor of New York, Theodore Roosevelt. He would be seen as a progressive candidate with widespread appeal. He would crucially be able to lock down New York's 39 electoral votes, the largest in the country at that time.

The results would be the same as 1904, with 336 electoral votes going to Roosevelt, and Democrat Alton Parker capturing 140 electoral votes.[6] The difference would be that Roosevelt would likely run for reelection in 1908. I can see him easily cruising to a second term if for no other reason than the Republicans at that time had a clear advantage in the Electoral College. The Democratic southern states alone were just not enough to carry a Democrat into the White House, especially with the Republican lock on New York State. That is why Democratic New York governors, like Martin Van Buren, Samuel J. Tilden, Grover Cleveland, Al Smith, and Franklin D. Roosevelt (FDR), were seen as solid choices as nominees.

With Roosevelt capturing a second term, that means no presidency for William Howard Taft. The election of 1912 would have been fascinating if President McKinley had survived assassination. Roosevelt, I suspect, would have been under enormous pressure to run for a third term. He would be 54 years old in 1912, hardly an old man.[7] In the actual results of the 1912 election it was Democrat Woodrow Wilson with 435 electoral college votes, Roosevelt 88, and Taft 8.[8] Taft, the incumbent president, had spent four listless, unremarkable years in the White House, leading to the Republican split in 1912 and his rejection at the polls.

Eight years of Roosevelt's energy and reforms would not be easy for the American people to turn away from. I think Theodore Roosevelt (TR) does run for a third term in 1912, which he was doing anyway in the real election of 1912. If he had no trouble with it in reality, I do not see what would stop him from wanting to stay in power. It is difficult to say if he would have defeated Wilson in 1912. Without the Republicans being split, it might have been an easier task. If he did defeat Wilson, that keeps him in the presidency until March 4, 1917, nearly three years into the outbreak of the Great War. Do the Americans enter World War I much sooner with TR as commander-in-chief? Or do they stay out of it longer? Roosevelt did win the Nobel Peace Prize in 1906 for his work ending the Russo-Japanese War.[9] It is difficult to say which direction he might have steered the country toward — peace or war. By the election of 1916, I could see him wanting to retire. His health was failing, so he likely would not run for a fourth term. Roosevelt died on January 6, 1919, at the age of 60.[10] Instead of Roosevelt seeking a fourth term in 1916, after two decades of Republicans I could see Democrat Woodrow Wilson winning in 1916, and guiding the country through the rest of the war.

How would the history of Buffalo have changed? If President McKinley had survived his assassination attempt, the gloom that it has placed on my city for well over a century would never have settled in. His trip there would have been seen as a triumph, the place where the president recovered, and went on to win a successful second term. The doctors who treated him would be hailed as heroes, and the Pan-American Exposition would be remembered as a City of Light, not a city of death.

Chapter 13

The Third Gun

The exact location where Leon Czolgosz purchased the gun to kill President McKinley has been wrongly reported for many decades now. I will take you through the process of how I determined the exact address of the place where he purchased the gun. I have already documented the suspicious nature of the assassin leaving for Cleveland on August 29 without a dime to his name, and returning to Buffalo on August 31 loaded with stacks of $50 bills.[1] That should arouse anyone's suspicions — that he could get that much money so quickly. No one really knows who he saw or what he did in Ohio. It is all conjecture. All that we do know is that he came back a wealthy man, and used that money to buy an expensive gun to shoot the president. I will examine the gun later. The first order of business is to determine where he bought the gun.

There are two books, other than mine, that are considered to be the authority on the history of the McKinley assassination. The first is *The Man Who Shot McKinley* by A. Wesley Johns, published in 1970 by A.S. Barnes and Company. The other is *Stolen Glory: The McKinley Assassination* by Jack C. Fisher, published in 2001 by Alamar Books.

This is what Johns writes about where Czolgosz purchased the gun: "the would-be Anarchist entered Walbridge Company's hardware store at 316 Main Street" to purchase the gun.[2] Fisher writes: "on September 3rd, Czolgosz entered the Walbridge Hardware Store at 316 Main Street" to purchase the revolver.[3] Both of them have the address wrong.

Then what is the correct address? A check of the Buffalo City Directory for 1901 is helpful. Pages 37 to 38 list all the addresses on Main Street. There is no listing for 316 Main Street. It did not exist.[4] And in 2022 it still does not exist. The approximate location on Google Maps if you search where that lot would be on Main Street in Buffalo is an area known as Cathedral Park, owned by St Paul's Episcopal Church. In fact, in 1901, it was not even Main Street in that spot. The address 316 Main Street was nowhere to be found. A different street went through the area. I owe a great deal of debt to Wayne A. Mori, the archivist for St Paul's, for determining that 316 Main Street did not exist. Here is how he explained the street pattern in 1901:

Professor Koerner,

For about 160 years Cathedral Park was known as Erie Street. In 1805, the street was called Vollenhoven St. If you like, I can provide you with an arial (*sic*) view of Erie Street c. 1960. In June of 1970, St. Paul's Cathedral, the City of Buffalo and Erie County signed an agreement to create a park-like area between Main and Pearl Streets. The area was landscaped, Erie St. was narrowed, and 63 Sycamores (London Plane Trees) were planted. St. Paul's owns only the lot (Lot 42) the present edifice stands on today. It never owned the picnic table and playground area. The new name, Cathedral Park, was given to Erie Street in 1971. Dedication and blessing of the park occurred on October 14, 1971. I believe that the playground was added in 1987, or there abouts.

All the best,
Wayne A. Mori, Archivist for St. Paul's Episcopal Cathedral[5]

The *Buffalo Courier* for June 9, 1900, has the answer for where Leon Czolgosz bought the murder weapon. It was an important day in the history of that store:

This morning the old and well-known wholesale and retail hardware firm of Walbridge and Co. will open to the public in its elegant new quarters, nos. 392 and 394 Main St....[T]he new building occupies a frontage of 50 feet in Main St. running through 283 feet to Pearl...The Main St. end of the building is 6 stories in height, while the Pearl St. end is seven stories.[6]

Like Garfield's assassin, this assassin chose to buy his gun in a place that also sold sporting goods. Therefore, we know exactly where in the store Czolgosz bought the gun. "Upon entering the store at the main entrance, one is confronted, on the left, first, with the sporting goods department, complete in every detail..."[7] Another check of the Buffalo City Directory for 1901 confirms this address. On page 102 of the Directory, under the "Buffalo Business Directory," "Walbridge and Co." is listed at "392–394 Main St."[8] According to Mori, Walbridge became Kobacker's sometime in the 1920s, and then was demolished to make way for the Main Place Mall in 1968.[9]

To summarize our findings, 316 Main Street in Buffalo did not exist in Buffalo in 1901 or at any point in time. We can say for certain that Leon Czolgosz walked into the first floor of Walbridge Hardware, at 392–394 Main Street, on September 3, 1901, and walked out with the weapon that would change history. We also know that the site where he bought the gun no longer exists. The gun, however, unlike Guiteau's, does exist, and it is time to examine the revolver used to murder the 25th president of the United States.

The gun used to assassinate McKinley was a .32-caliber Iver Johnson revolver, the same gun used by fellow anarchist Gaetano Bresci to kill Italy's King Umberto I on July 29, 1900.[10] Czolgosz kept a newspaper clipping of this assassination in his pocket nearly everywhere he went.[11] The gun has a muzzle force of 100 foot-pounds, and a velocity of 700 feet per second.[12]

He also purchased .32-caliber Smith and Wesson ammunition cartridges.[13] Gun historian Chris Eger pointed out that one of the features of this gun was how safe it was supposed to be:

Designed by fellow Scandinavian immigrant Andrew Fyrberg while at Iver Johnson and patented in 1896 under #566,393, [the weapon's] "Hammer the Hammer" action was positively revolutionary for handguns. Up until then you risked an accidental discharge from a dropped revolver if the gun was carried with a hammer down on a loaded cylinder, which as you may imagine, was a real concern at the time.

These guns were sold in both a small frame version with a three to six inch barrel in 22LR (7-shot) or 32S&W (5-shot), and a large frame 38S&W version that came in barrel lengths as short as 2-inches. With so many options you could buy a small concealable revolver for discreet carry or hiding in a cash drawer, or a larger piece for home defense.

When introduced [Iver Johnson] Safety Automatics retailed for $6, which in today's money is about $150. A nice, safe, and (for the time) relatively powerful handgun with a fast reload for a price that almost anyone could afford made it a hit for the company...

Some 250,000 First Model Iver Johnson Safety Automatics were made from 1894–96, a significant and brief production life if there ever was one. These guns use a single top latch to hold the revolver together, a simple design which boasts four patent dates listed on the barrel with the last one being '93. The first run of guns were all designed and built for low-pressure black powder cartridges...

The Second Model was made 1897–1908 and these were (generally) black powder only. They are identified easily due to the fact that they have a double top latch, a patent date that ends in '96, and serial numbers that start with letters A through F. Some 950,000 of these were produced. It was one of these; serial number 463344 bought for $4.50, that anarchist Leon Czolgosz shot President William McKinley with, in 1901.[14]

As for the ammunition for the gun, an interesting study was done on the bullets by the University at Buffalo School of Medicine in May 2000. This was similar to the study done on the bullets used in the Garfield assassination. The idea was to test the bullets to see if they were defective. Were they short of their gunpowder loads? The one that bounced off McKinley, two unfired bullets, and the three unspent casings were all weighed.[15] The results showed that one of the unspent bullets was short of its gunpowder load, "thus confirming," to put it in Fisher's words, "that Czolgosz had purchased defective ammunition. These findings also support the theory that one of the two cartridges fired was short its load, as first proposed in 1901 by a Buffalo police officer."[16]

Fisher did not make the following obvious point in his book, but if Czolgosz had loaded the gun in a different order with the two defective bullets first and second in the chamber, the president would have survived. If the ammunition package was ordered differently in the factory, placing the two defective bullets first and second to be taken out of the package, the president might have survived. If all the bullets were defective, he would have survived. This is the same thing that happened with Guiteau's gun. Some of his bullets were defective as well, but the devil himself was probably there with each assassin making sure they picked the "right" ones. It is almost too much to contemplate to think that the names Charles Guiteau and Leon Czolgosz would be footnotes to history if these men had just loaded their ammunition in a different order.

Chapter 14

Where Is the Gun That Killed McKinley?

If you look at how the gun is cataloged, with cold efficiency, at the Buffalo History Museum, you would think it was just any other artifact:

Object Name: Revolver
Catalog Number: 1963.413.1
Collection: Pan-American Exposition Collection
Date: ca. 1900
Description: Iver-Johnson, 32 caliber revolver, nickel plated except for the blued trigger guard. Top break action with automatic ejection. The serial number reads, "463344." The handle has hard rubber grips with conventional decoration surmounted by an owl's head. The ribbed barrel, Iver Johnson's Arms and cycle works, Fitchburg, Mass. USA/Pat's Apr. 6, 86, Feb. 5, 87, May 10, 87, Dec. 26, '98 Pat's pending. Several sets of initials have been engraved into the gun, ie: "LB/PVC (?)/FOB" The gun was used by Leon Czolgosz in the assassination of President William McKinley at the Pan-American Exposition on September 6, 1901 outside the Temple of Music.
Dimensions: H-7 W-4 inches
Material: Nickel-plated steel/rubber/metal
Credit Line: Penney, Hon. Thomas, Erie County District Attorney[1]

Strangely, the description says the gun was "outside the Temple of Music." This is not true. The shooting took place inside the Temple of Music, and the gun was pried from the assassin's hand after the second shot.[2]

I asked Walter Mayer Sr, Director of Museum Collections at the Buffalo History Museum, some questions about the gun. Here are my questions: Is the gun on display at the museum, and is it a replica? How long has it been on display? Do you have any of the unused bullets? How was the gun acquired, and when? Is there a receipt for when it was purchased by the assassin? Can it be photographed? Here are his answers:

No, the gun is the real one used. The gun was on display from 2001 to September of 2021 in the Pan-Am exhibit that has since closed. It's been in the exhibit Continuum since it opened in October of 2021. The Museum has three unused bullets, two used casings, and one spent bullet. The other [fatal] bullet is still in [buried with] McKinley. The gun was donated to the Museum by District Attorney Thomas Penney on 3/25/1902. To the best of my knowledge, a receipt for the purchase of the gun doesn't exist. Yes, you can take a photo of the gun on display.

Sincerely,
Walter Mayer, Sr., Director of Museum Collections[3]

The gun was not always on display, though. In January 2013, Anthony Greco, former Director of Exhibits for the Museum, gave an interview to Roadside America detailing more of the gun's history. Here is a portion of that interview:

A presidential assassin weapon is a conundrum for the museum that possesses it, mostly because of questions of when and how it's okay to display...One of the guns that almost killed Ford is showcased at his Presidential Museum in Grand Rapids, Michigan—but it's more curiosity than calamity since it didn't hurt anyone, and Ford himself gave the approval for its exhibit. That option wasn't available for the Buffalo History Museum in New York, which has preserved the gun that killed President McKinley since shortly after he was assassinated in 1901.

For a long time it was kept hidden from the public out of respect for the dead, said Anthony Greco, Director of Exhibits for the Museum. That self-imposed don't-exploit-a-tragedy exile ended years ago...But even the fake gun has been the target of thieves. "Our mission is to collect and preserve history," said Anthony. "Sharing only happens when we know we can preserve what we collect."

In other words, the real gun was too tempting a target. The gun is brought out for special occasions. A 150th museum birthday exhibit, running from 2012–2013, has exhumed not only the gun, but the bullets, the handcuffs slapped on the assassin, and the blood-spattered tea towel he used to hide the gun in his hand (The ball and chain later worn by the assassin are displayed all the time, evidently unappealing to relic-snatchers).

But when the celebration is over, the gun goes back in the closet. This doesn't make anyone happy. People want to see the real gun. The museum would like to show everyone the real gun.

"One of our goals right now is to try to find a way to get it on permanent display," said Anthony. Technology may make that possible. Moon rocks, for example, are now exhibited in bulletproof cases — or sometimes sealed inside protective pyramids — that are virtually indestructible and really, really hard to steal. There's no catalog where you can buy such a thing, but Anthony said he was looking into having a super-secure display case built for the gun. "Enough time has passed," he said. "It's something that people really want to see."[4]

For many years the gun was not on display, or a replica was used to keep away potential thieves. Thankfully, the gun can now be seen by anyone who visits the Buffalo History Museum, the former Pan-American Exposition New York State Building. It is on the second floor. The exhibit is fascinating. Of the four guns used to assassinate American presidents, only two are on public display: Lincoln's and McKinley's. The display at the Buffalo History Museum is shocking in its immediacy. The gun glistens in the light, looking pristine as if it has never been fired, with a picture of the Temple of Music beside it. Next to the display rests the white cloth the assassin used to conceal the gun. Also included in the exhibit are the surgical tools that were used in the failed effort to find the fatal bullet. The last piece in the exhibit is the ball and chains used to confine the prisoner as he awaited trial, conviction, and execution.

If you walk three blocks up Lincoln Parkway from the Buffalo History Museum, and make a left onto Fordham Drive, you will come across an equally important artifact. The rock marking the spot where the Temple of Music once stood, where that fatal shot rang out in 1901, sits unassumingly in the middle of the road. As with Garfield, the assassination site for McKinley does not exist anymore. Yet the echoes of those two gunshots from 1901 are still heard to this very day. My dear City of Buffalo still mourns your loss, President McKinley. May you rest in peace with your beloved Ida.

Part IV

The Assassination of President John F. Kennedy

Chapter 15

It Was Not Oswald

My approach here will be no different than with the other three assassinations. I would like to serve as a gateway to introduce a series of facts that will lead to obvious conclusions. I have some level of authority on this topic. My book *Why the CIA Killed JFK and Malcolm X: The Secret Drug Trade in Laos* (Chronos, 2014) was well received and the product of years of scholarly research. The mountain of evidence regarding the JFK assassination is intimidating. I will stick with my three stated goals, but they will take us in various directions. I will state the basic facts of the assassination, discuss the alleged murder weapons, and speculate on a second term for JFK.

The basic facts of the Kennedy assassination are as follows. President Kennedy was visiting Dallas, Texas, on November 22, 1963, to begin an early campaign swing through a key southern state he would need for reelection. He was accompanied by his wife, Jacqueline, and his vice president, Lyndon Johnson. Kennedy was riding in an open-topped car through Dealey Plaza at approximately 12:30 p.m. when he was shot a series of times. He was later pronounced dead, at approximately 1:00 p.m. Central Standard Time, at Parkland Memorial Hospital. Accused assassin Lee Harvey Oswald was shot by Jack Ruby on Sunday, November 24, 1963, and Oswald subsequently died later that day at Parkland Memorial Hospital.

I would like to start off with something easy to understand that might be shocking for those not familiar with the facts of this case. The reason Oswald was arrested and detained initially was that he was accused of killing Dallas Police Officer J.D. Tippit, which he denied. Oswald was arrested at the Texas Theater shortly before 2 p.m. on November 22, 1963.[1]

Butch Burroughs was the ticket taker and ran the concession stand at the Texas Theater. He also happened to be working on the day Tippit was shot, and saw Lee Harvey Oswald enter the theater. You can watch a video about this on YouTube. The title is "Witness: Oswald was in Texas Theater before 1:07." There is a link to it in the endnotes. In the video, Burroughs retells what he saw that day: "We were playing two movies called *War Is Hell* with Audie Murphy, and *Cry of Battle* with Van Heflin, and we started the movies at 1 o'clock, and I was counting candy behind the candy case, and he, Oswald, slipped in around between 1 and 1:07 [p.m.]."[2]

The Dallas Police Department Memorial Page lists the time of Tippit's shooting as 1:14 p.m.[3] His autopsy report lists his time of death as 1:15 p.m.[4] In other words, at the time that Tippit was being gunned down, Oswald had already "slipped into" the Texas Theater according to the primary witness who saw him enter, the ticket taker. This could have taken maybe an hour of police work to clear up: Go down to the theater, ask when Oswald entered, look at the time of Tippit's shooting, and then Oswald would have been immediately released on those trumped-up charges. Instead, he was kept in custody for a crime he physically never could have committed.

Before we get to Oswald's potential role in the assassination, we need to briefly chronicle the abundance of witness testimony that there was more than one person shooting at President Kennedy. Jim Marrs noted that "fifty-one witnesses placed shots in the vicinity of the Grassy Knoll. Several others believed shots were fired from locations other than those two [the Texas School Book Depository and the Knoll]."[5] Sixteen sheriffs' deputies "placed the origin of the shots near the triple underpass."[6] Also, four Dallas policemen thought the shots came from the Grassy Knoll, four said the Depository, and the other four did not have any opinion.[7]

Another indication that the president had been shot from the front, and not from the Texas School Book Depository where

Oswald was allegedly shooting, was the massive exit wound in the back of Kennedy's head. This was confirmed by doctors and nurses attending the dying president. These included Dr Paul Peters, Dr Kenneth Salyer, Dr Richard Dulaney, Dr Charles Carrico, Dr Ronald Jones, Dr Robert McClelland, Nurse Audrey Bell, and Dr Charles Crenshaw, all of whom confirmed the rear exit wound in subsequent interviews.[8] In the endnotes the reader will find a link to a full interview given by Dr McClelland where he details the full story of how he saw the exit wound in the back of the president's head in Trauma Room One at Parkland Hospital.[9]

From this information, we can draw some basic logical conclusions. First, Oswald did not kill Tippit. It would have been impossible for him to be at the scene of the shooting. Additionally, there are plenty of witnesses, backed up by forensic evidence, to indicate that more than one shooter was responsible for killing the president. With that in mind, it makes it even more important to know if it can be proven that Oswald was on the sixth floor of the Texas School Book Depository. Did he fire three precision shots at the president with a bolt-action Mannlicher-Carcano rifle?

One way to determine if someone has fired a gun is with a so-called "paraffin test." According to the *Merriam-Webster Dictionary*, a paraffin test is "a test in which a paraffin cast of the hand of a person suspected of firing a gun is subjected to chemical analysis to determine the presence of powder particles."[10] Mark Lane, an attorney from New York City, attempted to represent Oswald to the Warren Commission, but they denied him access. He tried to introduce evidence of Oswald's innocence, but they would not let him. "This case is full of falsehoods and contradictions," he said. "I know right now in the office of the Dallas district attorney there's a paraffin test which shows that Lee Harvey Oswald did not fire a rifle on November 22, 1963. I know that because I have a photostatic copy of that document."[11] Oswald's hands and cheeks were tested and no evidence of gunpowder was found.[12]

The fingerprint evidence linking Oswald to the murder weapon is also problematic. The FBI laboratory on November 23, 1963, examined the Mannlicher-Carcano, the alleged murder weapon. According to FBI Director J. Edgar Hoover, "No latent prints of value were developed on Oswald's revolver (*sic*), the cartridge cases, the unfired cartridge, the clip in the rifle, or the inner parts of the rifle."[13] The government found no fingerprints that could tie Oswald to the rifle. Later there would be the claim of a palm print that would link Oswald to it, but a palm print was not detected by the FBI on November 23, 1963, when Oswald was still alive. FBI expert Sebastian Latona said, "We had no personal knowledge of any palm print having been developed on the rifle."[14]

On Sunday afternoon, November 24, 1963, the rifle was flown back to Dallas after Oswald was pronounced dead. His body was sent to Miller Funeral Home in Fort Worth on the morning of Monday, November 25, 1963. In 1978, JFK assassination researcher Gary Mack confirmed that two FBI agents placed Oswald's palm print on the rifle that morning, "for comparison purposes."[15] Since Oswald had been fingerprinted three times at Dallas Police Headquarters there would be no need to do this unless it was done to tie him postmortem to the rifle.[16] Even Warren Commission member Lee Rankin said "there was a serious question in the minds of the commission as to whether or not the palm impression obtained from the Dallas Police Department is a legitimate latent palm impression..."[17]

The ammunition used in the Mannlicher-Carcano also indicated that it could not have come from Oswald. This from Jim Marrs:

The Mannlicher-Carcano ammunition raised questions about CIA involvement. According to an FBI document, the 6.5 mm ammunition found in the Texas School Book Depository was part of a batch manufactured on a U.S. government contract by Western Cartridge Corporation of East Alton, Illinois, which is now a part of Winchester-Western Division of Olin Industries. In the mid-1950s the Marine Corps purchased four million rounds of this ammunition, prompting the author of one FBI document to state "the interesting thing about this order is that it is for ammunition which does not fit and cannot be fired in any of the U.S. Marine Corps [USMC] weapons. This gives rise to the obvious speculation that it is a contract for ammunition placed by the CIA with Western Cartridge Corporation under a USMC cover for concealment purposes."[18]

There are also serious questions about Oswald being in the so-called "sniper's nest." Sheriff's Deputy E.L. Boone and Deputy Constable Seymour Weitzman spotted the alleged murder weapon first and wrote a report to the Dallas Police. They both were certain about what they had found. Weitzman wrote:

I was working with Deputy Boone of the Sheriff's Department and helping with the search. We were in the northwest corner of the sixth floor when Deputy Boone and myself spotted the rifle about the same time. This rifle was a 7.65 Mauser bolt action equipped with a 4/18th scope, a thick leather brownish black sling on it. The rifle was near the stairway. The time the rifle was found was 1:22 p.m.[19]

Dallas District Attorney Henry Wade also identified it as a "Mauser, I believe," in the early morning of November 23.[20] Dallas Police Chief Jesse Curry admitted that the rifle may have been switched, because no precautions were taken to lock it up in isolation. He said anyone "could have gotten away with it at the time." He even admitted the rifle in the National

Archives right now might not be the actual murder weapon.[21] Another rifle, a British Enfield .303, was found on the seventh floor of the Depository. It was seen being passed down the fire escape to Dallas Police just hours after the assassination, and photographed, but was never placed into evidence.[22]

Also, the idea of Oswald bringing the rifle into the building in a brown paper bag is full of holes as well. The brown bag he carried, according to the FBI, had no traces of gun or oil outlines that would fit the size of a Mannlicher-Carcano.[23] It is also impossible to tie Oswald to the acquisition of the gun, which was sent to his post office box but not signed by him. It was signed by Alex J. Hidell, in block letters.[24] We will also never know who had access to this post office box because the postal records were destroyed despite the requirement that they be saved for two years.[25]

The Mannlicher-Carcano was probably the worst weapon an assassin could have picked to shoot the president. The FBI described it as "cheap, defective, old, and flimsy."[26] Marrs asked the obvious question: "[A] defective gun managed to strike two men with three shots at a range of more than two hundred feet within six seconds?"[27] The scope of the Mannlicher-Carcano was sighted for a left-handed shooter, yet Oswald's brother and wife both insisted that he was right-handed.[28]

It is also nearly impossible to place Oswald on the sixth floor of the Texas School Book Depository at the time of the shooting at 12:30 p.m. He was seen in the second-floor lunchroom as late as 12:25 p.m. by secretary Carolyn Arnold. The Kennedy motorcade was running 15 minutes late due to an unscheduled stop. Oswald showed little concern about being in position to fire his weapon.[29] His alleged actions on the sixth floor truly stretch credulity. He allegedly fired three shots (choosing not to fire for some reason when the motorcade was coming up Houston Street, which was an easier shot), left three cartridges for the police to find in a neat row, wiped the rifle of fingerprints, wrapped it, hid it under some boxes, ran down five flights of stairs, and appeared in the lunchroom less than a minute after the assassination. Patrolman Marrion Baker rushed into the Depository and found Oswald in the lunchroom. Was Oswald out of breath? No. He was drinking a Coke "and didn't seem to be excited or afraid."[30]

Another huge problem with this is that at the time Oswald was supposedly making his escape down the back stairwell, employees Victoria Adams and Sandra Styles were also on the stairs. They never saw him. They had been watching the motorcade from the fifth floor, and saw the shooting. They decided to then take the stairs downstairs to see what was happening. They never saw Oswald on the stairs. There is a link in the endnotes to a full interview of their testimony.[31] They accurately note, as many other witnesses did, that the motorcade came to a stop. *The Girl on the Stairs: My Search for a Missing Witness to the Assassination of John F. Kennedy* (Create Space, 2011) by Barry Ernest is the authority on this topic.

An important addition to this story is the fact that their supervisor, Dorothy Garner, who was not interviewed by the Warren Commission, was with Adams and Styles during the assassination. She told the Department of Justice in June 1964 that she witnessed the two women walking downstairs soon after the shots were over. She stayed on the fifth floor.[32] Therefore, the obvious conclusion to draw is that Oswald was never on the sixth floor and was not the assassin, just as Oswald told the Dallas Police and reporters.

Chapter 16

The Fourth "Gun":
The Alleged Murder Weapon

What can we learn about the Mannlicher-Carcano as a weapon? Gun historian Ashley Hlebinsky offers this brief history, noting that there could have been other guns involved in the assassination:

The "Carcano" rifle was originally designed around 1890 by Salvatore Carcano, who was the chief technician at Turin Army Arsenal. It was made until the end of World War II and used by Italian troops in World War I and Italians and Germans in World War II. It's been used by other countries in conflicts as well. The original model was the 1891; it was an Italian bolt-action smokeless powder firearm. The Model 1891 has a sight that could range to 2,000 meters and a battle sight at 300 meters. The original barrel was long, which reflected a historic tradition that was effective for older military tactics. This type of warfare, however, was outdated by World War I. In response, many countries started developing the concept of a short rifle, including Italy.

In 1938, the Model 91 was modified and designated the Model 38. It has a shorter barrel of about 21 inches. The bolt handle was also turned down, and the rear sight was fixed with a 200 meter zero—a departure from the Model 91. Initially, it was chambered in 7.35x51mm, although after 1940, it was made in the original 6.5x52mm cartridge. This was the model owned by Oswald. But how did an Italian firearm made in 1940 end up in an American's hands decades later—especially with tightening restrictions in Italy on guns following World War II?

Throughout history, firearms have been used interchangeably for military and civilian purposes. Companies ramp up production during wartime, leaving large quantities of firearms available to be sold on the civilian market after the war ends. Oftentimes, these guns are sold at an inexpensive price. After the Civil War, for example, Springfield Rifled Muskets could be found for $6. That trend continued into the 20th century with Springfield Model 1903s and M1 Garands, to name a few, in the U.S. But this phenomenon happened around the world—and it included Carcano rifles.

Some Carcano rifles were sold by the Italian Army through the New York-based Adam Consolidated Industries. They were advertised for purchase in places like American Rifleman. The original advertisement Oswald saw didn't specify the model of Carcano. Initially, they were meant to be sold as Model 1891 TS carbines, but in 1962, the company couldn't acquire that model and swapped in Model 91/38s.[1]

The bolt of a Mannlicher-Carcano, according to JFK assassination expert Robert Groden, was

extremely difficult to work. No one, including the professional marksmen who later tried to duplicate the firing of the three successive shots with the Carcano, could have fired even two shots in 1.6 seconds and hit a target—especially a moving target. It was highly unlikely that Oswald was the marksman. Police, while searching through Oswald's possessions after his arrest, found no bullets for the 6.5 Mannlicher-Carcano rifle.[2]

Marrs notes that the Warren Commission left this FBI assessment of the Oswald gun out of its report:

FBI experts quoted firearms experts as calling the rifle "a cheap old weapon," "a very cheap rifle [which] could have been purchased for $3 each in lots of 25" and "a real cheap, common, flimsy-looking [gun]...very easily knocked out of adjustment." The FBI also noted that the Carcano was part of a gun shipment that was the subject of a legal proceeding by the Carlo Riva Machine Shop to collect payment for the shipment of rifles which Adam Consolidated Industries, Inc., claims were defective.[3]

Marrs also noted that Kennedy's death certificate states that he was killed by a "high powered," "high velocity" rifle. "Yet the Warren Commission stated the 6.5 mm Carcano only reached a velocity of less than 1,779 feet per second while a high velocity rifle exceeds 2,000 feet per second. Based on this discrepancy," said Marrs, "the Oswald rifle could not be the death weapon."[4] In addition, Marrs noted that the weapon was so decrepit that when the Army tested it, they needed three metal shims to adjust its scope, elevation, and azimuth.[5] J. Edgar Hoover also raised the possibility that there could have been more than one of those Carcanos with the same serial number out there because of how many were manufactured by Benito Mussolini in the 1930s.[6]

The Mannlicher-Carcano is now housed at the National Archives in College Park, Maryland. Can the rifle be viewed by the public? Here is the complicated answer to that question posted on their website:

Can I see the rifle or other artifacts?

It is NARA [National Archives and Records Administration] policy to make evidentiary objects available for viewing only when a researcher's needs cannot be met by a review of pictures, reproductions, or descriptions of the object and when production of the original will not cause damage or harm to the original. We will be glad to consider your request to see the physical evidence if you will:

1. Identify which specific exhibit or exhibits you wish to see. A general request to see all of the physical exhibits is not sufficient.
2. Indicate which of the photographs, drawings, measurements and descriptions of the exhibit and any other documentation relating to it you have examined.
3. Indicate briefly why the documentation available on the exhibit does not satisfy your research objectives and how those objectives might be met by observation of the original exhibits.

We will not consider any request unless the researcher has examined the digitized preservation photographs of the "Exhibits and Other Evidence from the President's Commission on the Assassination of President Kennedy (Warren Commission), 1959–1964" that are available through the National Archives Catalog.[7]

If you follow these instructions, search for "Mannlicher-Carcano Rifle Owned by Lee Harvey Oswald and Allegedly Used to Assassinate President John F. Kennedy."[8] There is a link to this page in the endnotes. There are five photographs of the rifle on the page. The first photo is "side view, bolt in front." The second photo is "side view, sling in front and bolt in back." The third photo is "close-up of butt plate of the rifle with the initials or mark." The fourth photo is "close up of scope. Photograph taken with a hand-held camera." The fifth photo is "close up of serial number (C2766) on the barrel of the rifle."[9]

There is an important additional instruction which makes your chances of seeing the physical gun close to zero:

Use Restriction(s): Restricted — Fully

Specific Use Restriction: Other

Note: It is the policy of the National Archives and Records Administration [NARA] to make evidentiary objects available for viewing only when a researcher's needs cannot be met by a review of photographs, reproductions, or descriptions of the object and when such viewing will not cause damage or harm to the original. We will be glad to consider your request to see the physical evidence if you will submit a written request to the reference staff for this series that:

1. Identifies which specific exhibit or exhibits you wish to see. A general request to see all of the physical exhibits is not sufficient.
2. Indicates which of the photographs, drawings, and descriptions of the exhibit and any other documentation relating to it you have examined.
3. Indicates briefly why the available documentation on the exhibit does not satisfy your research objectives and how those objectives might be met by observation of the original exhibits.[10]

It is interesting that this gun has never been in a museum. Perhaps it would be too tempting a target for a thief. The most revealing aspect, though, on the entire web page describing the gun is the word "Allegedly." In my opinion, the title should read: "Mannlicher-Carcano Rifle Possibly Never Owned by Lee Harvey Oswald and Probably Never Used to Assassinate President John F. Kennedy."

Chapter 17

Kennedy Survives Assassination Attempt in Dallas

There were many moments during the assassination when the president could have survived the attempt on his life. The first shot missed the motorcade. Kennedy and Texas Governor John Connally heard it and reacted to it. Connally turned to look at the president, while JFK stopped waving, turned his head, and looked at the Grassy Knoll.[1] At this point, someone should have known they were being shot at. Secret Service Agent Clint Hill, who was the closest to the car, should have recognized a gunshot and started running toward the president at this point. The president, a war veteran, should have hit the deck.

The second shot came from the front, and hit the president in the throat. JFK threw his arms up in obvious pain. Jacqueline Kennedy at this point should have known he was hit, and Clint Hill should have started running for the car. He still did not. The Secret Service also should have taken evasive action to get out of the shooting area. A neck wound is survivable. George Orwell, author of *1984*, survived one on May 20, 1937, during the Spanish Civil War. Although he experienced temporary paralysis, Orwell was eventually able to regain his voice and movement in his extremities.[2] JFK's ability to move his arms to his throat, with no visible signs of blood, implies that this shot had not hit an artery, or caused paralysis. If he had been rushed immediately to Parkland Hospital at this point, his chances of survival would have been high.

The fourth and fifth shots hit Kennedy in the back, causing him to lurch forward. These shots also hit Connally in the chest.³ Still, there was no reaction from the Secret Service or Jacqueline Kennedy to pull Kennedy out of danger. If the car had accelerated at this time, or taken evasive action, the president would have survived the assassination. Instead, the car came to a complete stop. This was seen by Victoria Adams and Sandra Styles, as noted above.⁴ It can also be seen in the Zapruder Film. I have included a link in the endnotes that details how the Zapruder Film, shot by amateur photographer Abraham Zapruder, was altered to disguise, among other things, this stoppage of the car during the fatal head shot. The two agents in the car lurch violently forward, as if the car has stopped, and a Dallas Police motorcycle catches up to the limousine, despite the car incongruously still moving forward.⁵

There were other shots that were aimed at Kennedy, but missed their target. These included shots that hit bystander James Tauge, who was standing near the triple underpass; a bullet hole in the windshield of the presidential limousine; a bullet in the grass on the south side of Elm Street; and a bullet near a manhole cover.⁶ With all these bullets flying around Dealey Plaza, many people have been led to be critical of the Secret Service reaction.

Senator Ralph Yarborough was riding with Vice President Lyndon B. Johnson and was very critical of the response of Secret Service agent and driver William Greer:

When the noise of the shot was heard, the motorcade slowed to what seemed to me a complete stop. After the third shot was fired, but only after the third shot was fired, the cavalcade speeded up, gained speed rapidly, and roared away to the Parkland Hospital. The cars all stopped...I don't want to hurt anyone's feelings but for the protection of future Presidents, they (the Secret Service) should be trained to take off when a shot is fired.⁷

Kenneth O'Donnell, a close Kennedy family friend and special advisor, was in the motorcade. O'Donnell was in the car directly behind the presidential limo in the Secret Service follow-up car, in the front seat, next to Secret Service Agent David Powers.[8] This gave him an unfettered view of the assassination. "If there was an interval of at least five seconds between the second and third shots, as it seemed, that was long enough for a man to run 50 yards," said O'Donnell. "If the Secret Service men in the front had reacted quicker to the first two shots at the President's car, if the driver had stepped on the gas before instead of after the fatal third shot was fired, would President Kennedy be alive today?"[9] The answer is yes.

One reason for their late reaction time may have been their late-night drinking session at a Fort Worth club, the Cellar, where many agents stayed until 3 a.m. on November 22, 1963.[10] In October 2014, *Vanity Fair* investigative reporter Susan Cheever looked into the question of whether the Secret Service could have saved JFK. Cheever confirmed the stories of Secret Service dereliction of duty:

> Six Secret Service members stayed at the Cellar until around three in the morning according to the letters they submitted to the Warren Commission. One of the men, Paul Landis, who would ride in the car behind the presidential limousine, wrote that he didn't leave until five A.M. "Every one of the agents involved had been assigned protective duties that began no later than eight A.M. on November 22, 1963," observed Philip Melanson, an expert on incidents of politically motivated violence, who would help oversee the archive of the Robert F. Kennedy assassination. Secret Service Agent Clint Hill told *Vanity Fair* that he left the Cellar before two A.M., went back to the hotel, and put in his breakfast order for six A.M. (He told the Warren Commission that he had stayed until 2:45 [a.m.].)[11]

Hill heard the first shot, but failed to react instantly, a mistake which cost the president his life. "I described it as an explosive device. It resembled a firecracker, but a loud one, and it came over my right shoulder from the rear," Hill said. "I wasn't absolutely sure what it was. I turned toward the noise."[12] He was not the only one who failed to react:

> Across from Hill, Agent Jack Ready was also on the footboards, yards from the president. Behind Ready, in similar proximity, was Paul Landis, also [like Hill] from Mrs. Kennedy's detail. "I knew right away it was a gunshot," Landis...[told] *Vanity Fair*, from his home near Cleveland, Ohio. "I was a hunter. I've done a lot of shooting. There was no doubt in my mind, in fact."[13]

Landis had stayed until 5 a.m. at the Cellar Club.[14] It also should be pointed out that other agents did recognize the first shot as gunfire, and reacted accordingly. This proves that Hill and Ready could have saved JFK's life if they had reacted the same way. From *Vanity Fair*:

> By way of contrast, the fourth car in the motorcade that day, containing Vice President Johnson and his wife, was guarded by other agents, including Rufus Youngblood. Youngblood had not joined the others at the Press Club and the Cellar the previous evening. And at the sound of the first shot, Youngblood, in line with his Secret Service training, pushed Johnson to the floor of the car and covered him with his own body.[15]

One of the people to expose this truth about Secret Service ineptitude was the first African American Secret Service agent, Abraham Bolden. This from *blackpast.org*:

On April 28, 1961, President John F. Kennedy, after a brief conversation with Bolden in Chicago, had him join the White House Secret Service Presidential Protective Division. From June 6, 1961 to July 6, 1961, Bolden traveled with and guarded President Kennedy. Following his probationary period, Bolden decided to return to Chicago as a field agent in the counterfeiting division.[16]

He was railroaded for trying to expose the truth about that night, and was pardoned in 2022 by President Joe Biden. This from *The Washington Informer* (April 26, 2022):

President Joe Biden announced Tuesday [April 26, 2022] that among his first pardons would be the first Black man to serve on a presidential detail, under President John F. Kennedy. Abraham Bolden was charged in 1964 with attempting to sell a copy of a Secret Service file. It took two trials to convict Bolden—the first resulted in a hung jury.

Bolden's conviction came after he claimed that he was framed for attempting to expose gross misconduct and speaking out against the continual racism he faced as a member of the Secret Service. During his second trial, witnesses admitted they were pressured by prosecutors into lying. Despite these admissions, Bolden was denied a new trial. Bolden remained unwavering in maintaining his innocence. He was sentenced to six years in federal prison, he served 39 months with a 2½-year probation.

Bolden wrote of his experiences in a 2008 book, *The Echo From Dealey Plaza*, in which he says the charges against him came only after he accused other agents assigned to President John F. Kennedy's detail of drinking the night before Kennedy's assassination in 1963 and being generally derelict in their duty.[17]

With so many chances the president had to survive the assassination, it makes this event even more tragic knowing he could have escaped Dealey Plaza wounded, without the fatal head shot. Yet, as with Lincoln, Garfield, and McKinley, the Secret Service agents at the moments they were most needed were nowhere to be found. The nation suffered the consequences.

Let us turn to what future was lost when President Kennedy died on that tragic day, November 22, 1963.

Chapter 18

President Kennedy Reelected in Landslide

There are two ways to look at the history of the United States with eight years of President Kennedy in office. The first has been done before, the idea of looking at the world as if the assassination never took place. That is not the approach I want to take. I think it is far more compelling to look at what would have happened if the president had survived the assassination, with the conspiracy playing out the same in Dealey Plaza. The only adjustment I will make is that the Secret Service agents react to the first shot, as they should have, and reach the motorcade just as JFK is being shot in the throat.

Here is what should have happened. Clint Hill hears the first shot. He recognizes immediately it is gunfire. The president stops waving, and turns his head. Hill begins running to the president's car. Just as he reaches the car, the president is shot in the throat. Hill climbs up and throws himself on the president. He pushes the president down to avoid the subsequent head shot. The other assassins keep firing at the car, hitting Hill in his right arm.

Seeing Hill sprinting to the car, and recognizing the sound of gunfire, Agent Jack Ready leaves his footboard immediately and begins running just behind Agent Hill, nearly matching his frantic pace. Ready leaps onto the car seconds after Hill, and absorbs a massive shot to his head, the one intended for the president. Other agents begin running for the presidential car as well. Hill administers cardiopulmonary resuscitation (CPR) on the president and closes the throat wound as best as he can with his hand. The limousine accelerates, and races down the Stemmons Freeway at over 100 miles an hour. Hill is screaming at Agent Greer to drive faster and to radio ahead to the hospital, as Agent Ready loses consciousness. As they reach the hospital, Agents Hill and Ready fall out of the car. It is mass confusion. Agents Kellerman and Greer assist Hill in taking the president out of the car. JFK is barely conscious and gasping for air. The president is rushed into Trauma Room One. He is given an emergency tracheotomy by Dr Charles Crenshaw to stabilize his breathing, and several blood transfusions, while lingering near death. The president regains consciousness around 1:30 p.m. when his vital signs stabilize. He is told not to talk, and rests through the night. Agent Hill is sent into emergency surgery. He later recovers after a brief convalescence. Agent Ready dies for his country, and his president, shortly after 1:00 p.m., from a massive exit wound in the back of his head. This is announced to the nation by Walter Cronkite around 1:30 p.m. Ready is later buried in Arlington National Cemetery with full military honors.

President Kennedy stays at Parkland Memorial Hospital for a month while his voice heals and he regains his strength. Messages pour in from citizens and world leaders, wishing the president a full recovery. President Kennedy returns to the White House on Christmas Eve to join the first lady and his family. His voice is still not fully recovered, but by the new year he resumes making his weekly radio address to ease back into public speaking.

Let us then examine what would happen for the remainder of his first term. He likely would make his first public speech to accept the Democratic nomination for a second term as president on August 27, 1964, at Atlantic City, New Jersey.[1] With all the outpouring of goodwill, the already popular president would no doubt cruise to a second term. He was already poised to get easily reelected months before the assassination, in March 1963. Here is what Pew Research found out about his job performance, and a potential matchup with Barry Goldwater, the eventual Republican nominee:

JFK was enormously popular in early 1963. In February, he enjoyed 70% approval. His ratings for handling foreign policy and handling domestic problems were equally high (64%) and most (56%) were satisfied with the way he was handling the situation in Cuba, where he had stumbled badly in 1961. And unlike modern presidents, Kennedy was a cultural phenomenon. In 1963, Gallup estimated that 85 million Americans had seen or heard a Kennedy imitator. In March 1963, 74% expected him to be reelected—he held a whopping 67%–27% lead over Barry Goldwater in a Gallup test election.[2]

If President Kennedy had survived his assassination attempt, 1964 would have been an interesting year for the United States, as a democratic republic. One thing that would be certain to happen is a completely different investigation into the attempted assassination—one that would lead to the truth, not a coverup. And the investigation would be led by JFK's ruthless brother, Attorney General Robert F. Kennedy. RFK would be hellbent on bringing to justice everyone who had tried to kill his brother. Many people do not realize he was doing exactly that in the years after the assassination. In fact, running for president in 1968 became a crusade to expose the truth.

This from JFK assassination experts David Talbot and Vincent Bugliosi (*Time*, June 21, 2007):

Bobby Kennedy would become America's first J.F.K. assassination-conspiracy theorist. The President's brother quickly concluded that Lee Harvey Oswald, the accused assassin, had not acted alone. And Bobby immediately suspected the CIA's secret war on Fidel Castro as the source of the plot. At his home that Friday afternoon, Bobby confronted CIA Director John McCone, asking him point-blank whether the agency had killed J.F.K. (McCone denied it.) Later, R.F.K.

ordered aides to explore a possible Mafia connection to the crime. And in a revealing phone conversation with Harry Ruiz-Williams, a trusted friend in the anti-Castro movement, Kennedy said bluntly, "One of your guys did it." Though the CIA and the FBI were already working strenuously to portray Oswald as a communist agent, Bobby Kennedy rejected this view. Instead, he concluded Oswald was a member of the shadowy operation that was seeking to overthrow Castro.

Bobby knew that a dark alliance—the CIA, the Mafia and militant Cuban exiles—had formed to assassinate Castro and force a regime change in Havana. That's because President Kennedy had given his brother the Cuban portfolio after the CIA's Bay of Pigs fiasco. But Bobby, who would begin some days by dropping by the CIA's headquarters in Langley, Va., on his way to the Justice Department, never managed to get fully in control of the agency's sprawling, covert war on Castro. Now, he suspected, this underground world—where J.F.K. was despised for betraying the anti-Castro cause—had spawned his brother's assassination.

As Kennedy slowly emerged from his torment over Dallas and resumed an active role in public life—running for U.S. Senator from New York in 1964 and then President in 1968—he secretly investigated his brother's assassination. He traveled to Mexico City, where he gathered information about Oswald's mysterious trip there before Dallas. He met with conspiracy researcher Penn Jones Jr., a crusading Texas newspaperman, in his Senate office. He returned to the Justice Department with his ace investigator Walter Sheridan to paw through old files. He dispatched trusted associates to New Orleans to report to him on prosecutor Jim Garrison's controversial reopening of the case. Kennedy told confidants that he himself would reopen the investigation into the assassination if he won the presidency, believing it would take the full powers of the office to do so. As Kennedy adviser Arthur Schlesinger Jr. once observed, no one of his era knew more than Bobby about "the underground streams through which so much of the actuality of American power darkly coursed: the FBI, CIA, the racketeering unions and the Mob." But when it came to his brother's murder, Bobby never got a chance to prove his case.[3]

If the president survived the assassination, the Kennedys would want to know who was behind it. They would want to know the truth, and publicly bring all the conspirators to justice. This would be for a simple reason—so it would not happen again. The president would fear for his life and refuse to go out in public until he knew what forces were trying to kill him. Only then could he safely live out the rest of his terms in office. He would likely task the Justice Department to head up the investigation to see who was behind this. Robert Kennedy's instincts were correct. His investigation would have led him to the Central Intelligence Agency (CIA). This would likely take months to do, but it would be easier because they would not be starting from the premise of a lie. JFK would suspect that it was the CIA who were conspiring to kill him. The tension with that agency went back to the Bay of Pigs Invasion.

Since the Bay of Pigs, the CIA had developed plans to retaliate, and one such plan included trying to destroy the Peace Corps. The Corps was established by executive order on March 1, 1961, to promote peace, fight third-world poverty, and promote the idea of civic service to the United States.[4] The CIA plan to turn an agency designed to promote peace into an agency designed to start wars was diabolical. Kennedy had a conversation with Sargent Shriver, Peace Corps Director, on April 2, 1963, about this issue. Shriver telephoned JFK because he suspected a group of new recruits "looked suspicious" and were probably undercover CIA agents. The Corps had already rejected many applicants who worked for the CIA.[5] Kennedy responded that he was "very anxious about this," and such an infiltration could ruin and "discredit" the whole purpose of the Peace Corps.[6] Kennedy speechwriter Theodore Sorenson said that the Peace Corps had to work exhaustively to keep the Corps free of agents in its early years.[7] Corps organizers had to worry about CIA operatives approaching corps members to enlist them as undercover agents who could secretly infiltrate the agency. New recruits were told to report all contact to their supervisors.[8]

Because of this history of trying to use the Peace Corps as a CIA front to promote war, there is still a lack of trust within the Corps toward that agency. "If you have ever worked for the CIA, you are permanently ineligible for employment at the Peace Corps. Do not submit an application for employment with the Peace Corps," reads the "Eligibility" section on the Peace Corps website. "If you currently live with someone who works for the CIA, you will not be eligible for employment with the Peace Corps until you have ceased living with that person for at least six months. Do not submit an application for employment with the Peace Corps until that waiting period has elapsed."[9]

The faceoff with the CIA continued. Kennedy was forced to take decisive action. He decided to remove the covert operations power of the CIA and have all decisions go directly through him. On June 28, 1961, JFK issued National Security Action Memorandums 55, 56, and 57. These were orders by the commander-in-chief to restructure the entire military-industrial complex. Kennedy ordered that covert paramilitary operations of the CIA were to be shifted to the Department of Defense and the Joint Chiefs of Staff. In NSAM 55, JFK stated that:

a. I regard the Joint Chiefs of Staff as my principal military advisor responsible both for initiating advice to me and for responding to requests for advice. I expect their advice to come to me direct and unfiltered.

b. The Joint Chiefs of Staff have a responsibility for the defense of the nation in the Cold War similar to that which they have in conventional hostilities. They should know the military and paramilitary forces and resources available to the Department of Defense, verify their readiness, report on their accuracy, and make appropriate recommendations for their expansion and improvement. I look to the Chiefs to contribute dynamic and imaginative leadership in contributing to the success of the military and paramilitary aspects of Cold War programs.[10]

The Joint Chiefs of Staff would now be the "principal military advisor," not the CIA. The advice to the president must be "direct and unfiltered," implying that in the past the CIA had lied to JFK and hidden information from him. The president was also saying that he was now counting on the Chiefs' leadership in "paramilitary" operations, an area that had been assigned to the CIA until then. This World War II veteran was trying to reestablish the model of "conventional" warfare that existed during World War II when there was no CIA, and the president and the Chiefs operated in tandem. NSAM 55 was a devastating blow to the power, influence, and role of the CIA. So was NSAM 57, issued that same day. Here is how it read, in part:

Any proposed paramilitary operation in the concept state will be presented to the Strategic Resources Group for initial consideration and for approval as necessary by the President. Thereafter, the SRG will assign primary responsibility for planning, for interdepartmental coordination and for execution to the task force, department or individual best qualified to carry forward the operation to success, and will indicate supporting responsibilities. Under this principle, the Department of Defense will normally receive responsibility for overt paramilitary operations. Where such an operation is to be wholly covert or disavowable, it may be assigned to CIA, provided that it is within the normal capabilities of the agency. Any large paramilitary operation wholly or partly covert which requires significant numbers of military trained personnel, amounts to military equipment which exceed normal CIA-controlled stocks and/or military experience of a kind and level peculiar to the Armed services is properly the primary responsibility of the Department of Defense with the CIA in a supporting role.[11]

These directives from the commander-in-chief meant that the CIA was now going to have to move through several oversight bodies before its operations could get approved, including the Strategic Resources Group, the Department of Defense, and, most importantly, the president himself. Large paramilitary operations would now be handled by the Department of Defense, and the CIA would only have a "supporting role" in operations.

Tension with the agency did not end there. Kennedy's efforts for peace in Laos and Vietnam would end CIA access to the opium/heroin market that would eventually spread to South America. His shutting down of Operation Northwoods in March 1963 was another clashing point with the CIA, as well as with the Joint Chiefs of Staff. Their plan was to stage fake acts of domestic terrorism, blame them on Fidel Castro, and use this as a pretext to invade Cuba.[12]

The research of Jim Marrs, Jim Garrison, and the revelations of E. Howard Hunt have uncovered what role the CIA planned in the JFK assassination and its coverup. Hunt was a member of the CIA almost from its inception. He was also a key part of Richard Nixon's plumbers who covered up leaks in the Watergate scandal. Hunt died on January 23, 2007.[13] Before he passed away, Hunt made a series of deathbed confessions to his son, St. John. Hunt revealed the names and involvement of members of the CIA in the assassination of JFK. Here is who he said was involved:

1. CIA Agent David Morales. Died in 1978 before he could be questioned by the House Select Committee on Assassinations. Like Hunt, he worked on the Bay of Pigs Invasion fiasco, and blamed Kennedy for its failure. Recruited French assassin Lucien Sarti to be the sniper on the so-called "grassy knoll" to deliver the kill shot. Importantly Morales is a link to the Southeast Asian drug trade, having served the agency both in Laos and Vietnam. He later bragged to a friend about the assassination saying, "We took care of that son of a bitch, didn't we?"

2. CIA Agent Frank Sturgis. Worked with Hunt and other agents in covert operations in Cuba and Watergate, saying the break-in at Democratic headquarters in June 1972 was part of the cover-up of the JFK assassination. He also served as a link between the Mafia and the agency. Like Hunt, he was likely in Dallas on the day of the assassination, captured by the *Dallas Morning News* as one of the three "tramps."

3. Antonio Veciana. CIA contract agent who failed in his attempt to kill Castro. Testified in front of Congress that he saw his CIA contact, David Atlee Phillips, traveling with Lee Harvey Oswald in Dallas in the summer of 1963.

4. CIA Agent David Atlee Phillips. Involved with Hunt and Sturgis in the failed Bay of Pigs Invasion. Phillips was the Mexico City CIA Station Chief when it was allegedly visited by Oswald, who he was later seen with in September 1963 in Dallas. Recruited Veciana and agent William K. Harvey into the plot. Went on to become CIA operations chief in Latin America where he helped to organize a successful assassination plot against a Chilean politician in 1970.

5. CIA Agent William K. Harvey. Longtime leader of clandestine operations and yet another link between the CIA and the Mafia. In 1960 he was selected to lead a covert CIA assassination team named ZR-RIFLE. He harbored bitter resentment toward JFK for his policies of peace, such as not invading Cuba...He died in 1976 before he could testify in front of the House.

6. CIA Agent Cord Meyer. In charge of "Operation Mockingbird," the CIA domestic propaganda program that, among other goals, pushed the myth of the Domino Theory on the public. This was the unproven theory that if one nation fell to communism, all other nations would fall like a row of dominoes, and also become communist. Mockingbird enlisted domestic and foreign journalists to push the CIA agenda both at home and abroad through misinformation and infiltration of various groups. The selling of the Domino Theory, beginning in the 1950s by the CIA, was key to convincing the public to support their various covert operations throughout the world, especially in Southeast Asia. Meyer's former wife, Mary, was a mistress of JFK. She was mysteriously killed in 1964. Cord Meyer was likely the group leader, coordinating the plot to kill Kennedy.[14]

We also know after years of research by many historians that another area of involvement of the CIA, which can be proven, is that they covered up evidence, primarily by altering the Zapruder Film. I have included a link in the endnotes to a video that explains all the various changes they made.[15] These included taking out the stoppage of the car and blacking out the back of the president's head to disguise the exit wound. CIA photo analyst Dino Brugioni gave an interview to author Douglas Horne on January 14, 2014 about this. There are two links to this in the endnotes. Brugioni detailed how the

Secret Service handed him the film to be worked over at the Hawkeye Plant in Rochester, New York, on the evening of November 23, 1963. The original film showed a bullet hole in the Stemmons Freeway sign, a full stoppage of the car, a massive blood spray above the president's head, and a large exit wound in the back of his head.[16] The ammunition in the alleged murder weapon was also CIA stock ammunition, as noted above.[17]

Keep in mind that the CIA was developed for the Cold War and was relatively new in the 1960s. The agency is not in the Constitution. If JFK was trying to end the Cold War, the CIA was in danger of becoming obsolete. No matter how long it would take, an investigation by Attorney General Robert Kennedy would lead to the prosecution of all agents who took part in the plot to kill the president. There would be public trials for treason. The definition of treason is "the offense of attempting by overt acts to overthrow the government of the state to which the offender owes allegiance or to kill or personally injure the sovereign or the sovereign's family."[18] Article 3, Section 3, of the United States Constitution states: "Treason against the United States, shall consist only in levying War against them, or in adhering to their Enemies, giving them Aid and Comfort. No Person shall be convicted of Treason unless on the Testimony of two Witnesses to the same overt Act, or on Confession in open Court."[19]

If the standard was too high for treason, conspiracy to murder the president might be an easier lift. Some agents would trade immunity for revealing the details of the conspiracy. Robert Kennedy would not rest until every single person who tried to kill his brother was in jail. And with JFK safely running the executive branch, there would be nothing that could stop them. All of the men listed above would be sent to prison, some executed for treason. The president would completely dismantle the agency and move all covert operations to the Department of

Defense. Defense Secretary Robert McNamara was one of the few people he could trust, outside of his brother.

After JFK was safely reelected, the trials would begin in 1965 once all the evidence was gathered. In the meantime, many involved in the conspiracy would mysteriously die before trial, but either way the truth would come out that the CIA had tried to kill their own commander-in-chief.

With the CIA neutered, exposed, and dismantled, the agency would then be unable to assassinate Malcolm X, Martin Luther King, and Robert Kennedy. Let us take stock of the implications of this. The president wanted to shatter the CIA "into a thousand pieces and scatter them to the winds."[20] If RFK and JFK were to eventually find out that the agency tried to kill the president, there is no way they would let them continue to exist, to again threaten their lives. The CIA trials would also spell the end of the agency's effort to expand the drug trade in Southeast Asia. With a dismantled, treasonous agency out of the way, the president could easily disengage from Laos and Vietnam. The point I am making is that if JFK had been president in his second term, February 21, 1965 (death of Malcolm X), April 4, 1968 (death of Martin Luther King), and June 6, 1968 (death of Robert Kennedy), would have been days that passed just like any other days on the calendar. Additionally, the Vietnam War would have ended in 1965, which, I posit, is the primary reason these three men were assassinated. Did the CIA kill these men?

For Malcolm X

In the late 1960s, television news reporter Louis Lomax got the idea of doing a movie exploring the life of Malcolm X. Earlier in his career he had teamed up with another reporter named Mike Wallace to do a documentary about the Nation of Islam and Malcolm X. It was titled *The Hate That Hate Produced*. It aired on June 13, 1959. Lomax maintained an interest in the black Muslim leader, and a few years after Malcolm X's death he began producing a full-length feature film about the life and death of this Black Power icon. The main focus was how the Central Intelligence Agency played a primary role in the Malcolm X assassination. This movie never made it to air. Lomax died on July 31, 1970, in a car crash. His brakes had mysteriously been cut. He was on his way to the production studio at the time of this fatal "accident."[21]

The illegal surveillance, harassment, and bombing of his home led Malcolm X to believe that the Nation of Islam (which he had recently cut ties from) could not be responsible for all the constant threats to his life and the lives of his family members. "The more I keep thinking about this thing," he told author Alex Haley, who was helping him write his autobiography, "the things that have been happening lately, I'm not at all sure it's the Muslims. I know what they can do, and what they can't do, and they can't do some of the stuff recently going on."[22]

At the time of Malcolm X's assassination, he was being closely monitored by the FBI Director, the CIA Director, the CIA's Deputy Director of Plans (responsible for covert actions and assassinations), the Director of Naval Intelligence, the Chief of the Air Force Counterintelligence Division, and the Army's Assistant Chief of Staff for Intelligence.[23] This was almost the entire intelligence apparatus of the Federal Government.

There are two specific incidents that have indications of CIA involvement. The first happened on July 23, 1964, just seven months before his assassination. Malcolm X was in Cairo, Egypt, to address the Organization of African Unity Conference. He was going to present a petition seeking cooperation in his effort to bring US human rights violations before the United Nations. Malcolm X was having dinner at the Nile Hilton Hotel in Cairo. This was the night before his scheduled speech, which was to take place on July 24, 1964. In his entourage was New York City Councilman Milton Henry. Malcolm X and Henry noticed two white men sitting nearby watching them eat. The two men had been stalking them all day. "There was one agent who especially irritated Malcolm," Henry said. "We couldn't eat without him being at the next table."[24] Suddenly Malcolm X got violently ill. "He would have died," Henry said, "if we had not been able to get him to the hospital in a hurry."[25]

After he was rushed to the hospital, doctors immediately pumped his stomach. The contents were sent for analysis. The results indicated that someone had placed a "toxic substance" in the food of Malcolm X. The doctors insisted that the chance that the food was naturally tainted by something like botulism was "nil."[26] An attempt was made to find the waiter who had served Malcolm X and Henry, but he mysteriously could not be found. "Someone deliberately tried to poison me," Malcolm X said. It would not have been the first time the CIA tried to poison someone. Other examples of CIA poisoning plots include attempts on Congo leader Patrice Lumumba in 1960, Cuban dictator Fidel Castro throughout the 1960s, and Chinese Premier Chou En-lai in 1955 at the Afro-Asian Conference in Bandung.[27]

Despite this attempt at killing him, Malcolm X submitted his petition to the conference anyway. He received widespread support to "internationalize the American Negro problem so as to accentuate the struggle," he said. "This can only be done by linking the fate of the new African states with that of the American Negroes."[28] Malcolm X also pledged to form a coalition with Martin Luther King so they spoke as a single voice on African issues. Nothing was going to stop Malcolm X in his struggle for human rights, except death. Malcolm X knew he was a marked man, though, saying: "I will never get old."[29]

And then just 12 days before his assassination, another incident took place that solidified his thinking on who was trying to kill him. "The more I keep thinking about what happened to me in France," he later told Alex Haley, "I think I'm going to quit saying it's the Muslims."[30] On February 9, 1965, Malcolm X flew to Orly Airport in Paris for a speaking engagement. Instead, being unable to gain entry to the country, he was immediately surrounded by French police and told to return home.[31] He was forced to fly back to London and eventually back to the United States. Malcolm X was confused by this because he had just spoken in France three months before and this country was a democracy with a free press. Why was he being treated like a criminal?

In April 1965, a journalist named Eric Norden, who was researching the assassination, received the answer as to why Malcolm X could not enter France. Norden was told by an African diplomat that his country's intelligence agency "had been quietly informed by the French Department of Alien Documentation and Counter-Espionage that the CIA planned Malcolm's murder and France feared he might be liquidated on its soil." French intelligence had passed this information to the diplomat because his North African country was a nation that Malcolm had visited recently, to much acclaim. French agents thought that perhaps, after being denied entry into Paris, the black leader might choose to revisit that North African nation, and if so, its government needed to be ready for the CIA to carry out the plot against his life on African soil.[32]

Author James W. Douglass said: "Malcolm realized that…the Nation of Islam [NOI] was now serving as a proxy, much like how the CIA used the Mafia as their go-between in the attempted killing of Castro." The use of hired NOI assassins in the shooting of Malcolm X (most of whom escaped the crime scene and have never been identified) "furnished a plausible deniability and a showy scapegoat," Douglass wrote. This was a counterintelligence operation planned at high levels of the US government, a "joint FBI-CIA operation, [and] the Nation of Islam was being used as a religious Mafia."[33]

We also know, since 2021, that the alleged assassins of Malcolm X were finally set free after 50 years of being wrongly accused of this murder. This from the *New York Post* (November 21, 2021):

> Two men convicted in the assassination of Malcolm X more than five decades ago are set to finally be exonerated after professing their innocence since his murder, their lawyers and the Manhattan District Attorney's Office said Wednesday.
>
> Muhammad Aziz, 83, and the late Khalil Islam—who both spent decades in prison—will have their convictions tossed on Thursday, following a nearly two-year investigation into the 1965 killing of the civil rights leader.
>
> "The events that brought us here should never have occurred," Aziz said in a statement. "Those events were and are the result of a process that was corrupt to its core—one that is all too familiar—even in 2021."
>
> "While I do not need a court, prosecutors, or a piece of paper to tell me I am innocent, I am glad that my family, my friends, and the attorneys who have worked and supported me all these years are finally seeing the truth we have all known, officially recognized," he said.
>
> The renewed probe unearthed evidence of the two men's innocence that had been hidden from the defense at their trial by the FBI and the NYPD [New York Police Department], according to their attorneys, the Innocence Project and civil rights lawyer David Shanies.[34]

The effort to find out the truth about CIA involvement in the Malcolm X assassination has extended to his surviving family. This from *Reuters* on February 21, 2023:

A daughter of Malcolm X, the civil rights activist assassinated 58 years ago to the day on Tuesday, has filed notices that she intends to sue the FBI, the CIA, New York City police and others for his death.

Ilyasah Shabazz accused various federal and New York government agencies of fraudulently concealing evidence that they "conspired to and executed their plan to assassinate Malcolm X."

"For years, our family has fought for the truth to come to light concerning his murder," Shabazz said at a news conference at the site of her father's assassination, now a memorial to Malcolm X.[35]

Hopefully these efforts at exposing the truth will prevail.

For Martin Luther King

In 1999 the King family conducted a mock trial on the HBO cable TV channel where, over the course of 30 days, 70 witnesses testified under oath that the CIA and the military conspired to assassinate Dr King in 1968.[36] They acquitted patsy James Earl Ray of the crime. To summarize the conclusions of decades of investigation by attorney William Pepper: On April 4, 1968, there were two teams of assassins ready to eliminate Dr King. One was controlled by the local Memphis Mafia, with help from the Memphis Police. The other was a trained CIA/military team waiting, with high-powered rifles, as a backup plan at a remote location in case the first team failed, which they did not. Pepper's book, *An Act of State* (Verso, 2008), details the plot.

For Robert Kennedy

Sirhan Sirhan, the convicted assassin of Robert Kennedy, has since come forward and claimed that he was brainwashed by the CIA's MKUltra program.

"There is no question he was hypno-programmed," lawyer William F. Pepper told ABCNews.com. "He was set up. He was used. He was manipulated."...

Pepper plans to introduce new evidence that suggests there was a second gunman who fatally shot RFK in the kitchen of a Los Angeles hotel, following his victory in the 1968 California presidential primary...

Pepper said he believes Sirhan was "hypno-programmed," essentially brainwashed to kill Kennedy and his memories were then erased...

"Ten independent witnesses say Sirhan was always in front of Bobby, never behind him," said Pepper, "but the autopsy says Bobby was shot at close range from behind the right ear."...

Pepper said Sirhan is "remorseful" for his role in the 1968 assassination of Kennedy, but the gunman "does not remember anything about the shooting."[37]

One of those witnesses who came forward stating that there was more than one gunman was Nina Rhodes-Hughes. This from the *Huffington Post* (April 30, 2012):

Nina Rhodes-Hughes, a key witness to the Robert F. Kennedy assassination at the Ambassador Hotel in 1968, is making bombshell claims in a CNN interview, suggesting that convicted murderer Sirhan Sirhan didn't act alone.

"What has to come out is that there was another shooter to my right," Rhodes-Hughes, who was feet away from RFK in a hotel service pantry during the crime, told CNN. "The truth has got to be told. No more cover-ups."

Rhodes-Hughes, now 78, claims the FBI "twisted" her statements to investigators after the incident in order to come up with the conclusion that she had only heard 8 shots, an account that was used as evidence that Sirhan carried out the act without an accomplice.

With Sirhan's legal team now revisiting the case, however, Rhodes-Hughes is coming forward with concrete allegations. "I never said eight shots. I never, never said it," she told CNN, accusing California Attorney General Kamala Harris of inaccurately "parroting" the incorrect information on the original FBI report. "There were more than eight shots...There were at least 12, maybe 14. And I know there were because I heard the rhythm in my head."[38]

The point I am making is that if President Kennedy had survived assassination, uncovered the truth, and dismantled the CIA, these assassinations would never have taken place. Entire books can be written on what the world would look like if Malcolm X, King, and RFK had been allowed to live out the rest of their lives. The implications of that are enormous. Malcolm X and King may have formed an alliance, finding common ground in King's planned "Poor People's Movement." RFK would likely run for president at some point, perhaps winning in 1968 after eight successful years serving in his brother's administration. This would spare the nation the Watergate scandal in the Nixon administration, and the Kent State shootings. The US would enjoy the leadership of three civil rights leaders who would likely live into the 1990s. I could potentially see King getting appointed to the Supreme Court under an RFK administration.

Having dealt with the CIA, the Kennedy brothers would likely move on to uncover who else was involved in the plot, or who had prior knowledge and did nothing to stop it. The finger of suspicion would eventually point to Lyndon Johnson, and for good reason.

On November 21, 1963, the night before the assassination, there was a gathering at the Dallas mansion of oil magnate Clint

Murchison Sr. Guests in attendance included Vice President Lyndon Johnson, FBI Director J. Edgar Hoover, former Vice President Richard Nixon, and other Texas oil businessmen who were friends of Murchison. The oilmen in Texas hated Kennedy's policy of ending the Oil Depletion Allowance. As a Texas senator, Johnson was a major supporter of the Oil Depletion Allowance, which allowed companies to avoid paying taxes on the wealth they and their families obtained from oil.[39]

As Robert Bryce explained in his book, *Cronies: Oil, the Bushes, and the Rise of Texas, America's Superstate*: "Numerous studies showed that the oilmen were getting a tax break that was unprecedented in American business. While other businessmen had to pay taxes on their income regardless of what they sold, the oilmen got special treatment." Bryce gave an example of how the Oil Depletion Allowance worked:

An oilman drills a well that costs $100,000. He finds a reservoir containing $10,000,000 worth of oil. The well produces $1 million worth of oil per year for ten years. In the very first year, thanks to the depletion allowance, the oilman could deduct 27.5 per cent, or $275,000, of that $1 million in income from his taxable income. Thus, in just one year, he's deducted nearly three times his initial investment. But the depletion allowance continues to pay off. For each of the next nine years, he gets to continue taking the $275,000 depletion deduction. By the end of the tenth year, the oilman has deducted $2.75 million from his taxable income, even though his initial investment was only $100,000.[40]

This benefited all the oilmen in Texas, including Murchison.

President Kennedy had other ideas about the Oil Depletion Allowance. According to JFK assassination researcher, John Simkin:

On 16th October, 1962, Kennedy was able to persuade Congress to pass an act that removed the distinction between repatriated profits and profits reinvested abroad. While this law applied to the industry as a whole, it especially affected the oil companies. It was estimated that as a result of this legislation, wealthy oilmen saw a fall in their earnings on foreign investment from 30 per cent to 15 per cent.[41]

Kennedy then went further during his State of the Union Address, on January 17, 1963, waging a full attack on the Oil Depletion Allowance:

President Kennedy presented his proposals for tax reform. This included relieving the tax burdens of low-income and elderly citizens. Kennedy also claimed he wanted to remove special privileges and loopholes. He even said he wanted to do away with the oil depletion allowance. It is estimated that the proposed removal of the oil depletion allowance would result in a loss of around $300 million a year to Texas oilmen.

In presenting the tax reform proposal, Kennedy said that "no one industry should be permitted to obtain an undue advantage over all others..."[42]

As Lyndon Johnson was leaving the Murchison mansion late that night, on November 21, 1963, he was confident enough to tell his mistress, Madeline Duncan Brown, who was also there, something quite ominous. Johnson said, "Those goddamn Kennedys will never embarrass me again. That is no threat. That is a promise." He repeated the threat in a phone call to her the following morning, just hours before the assassination. She wrote about this in her 1997 book, *Texas in the Morning*. JFK assassination filmmaker Nigel Turner extensively covers the existence of the meeting in Murchison's house, and the proof for it, in part nine of his documentary *The Men Who Killed*

Kennedy. He interviewed Brown, as well as May Newman, a seamstress for Clint's wife, Virginia. Newman confirmed that the Murchison chauffeur drove Hoover back and forth from the airport, and that the stingy FBI Director stiffed him on the tip both times.[43]

I have included a link in the endnotes to the episode "The Guilty Men," which details all the evidence against Lyndon B. Johnson (LBJ).[44] The title is "Kennedy Assassination – Lyndon Johnson Killed JFK – The Men Who Killed Kennedy." This episode was banned for many years due to its controversial information. The documentary points to two other areas that could tie Johnson to the assassination. One is the potential for him to go to jail, and the other is a fingerprint found in the Texas School Book Depository on the day of the assassination. This from LBJ historian Phillip F. Nelson:

Lyndon Johnson was also behind the infamous "TFX Scandal" —a story merely summarized here, but meticulously detailed within "LBJ The Mastermind..." —for which Johnson had collected at least one known (probably more) suitcase filled with $100,000 in cash. This scandal was the result of his clever plot that caused the cancellation of a government contract to Boeing (Washington state based) so that it could be given to General Dynamics (Texas based). For that, he was assisted by a number of others, including Fred Korth, Secretary of the Navy (who was forced to resign his position due to the unfolding scandal), Deputy Secretary of Defense Roswell Gilpatrick, and Robert McNamara, Secretary of Defense.

The intensity of questioning these officials in the weeks leading up to JFK's assassination is reflected in this vignette: During chairman John McClellan's Senate Investigations Subcommittee hearings, which was then engaged in investigating the granting of the TFX contract to General Dynamics, Senator Sam Ervin asked Robert McNamara:

"...whether or not there was any connection whatever between your selection of General Dynamics, and the fact that the Vice President of the United States happens to be a resident of the state in which that company has one of its principle, if not its principle, office."

McNamara tearfully responded, "Last night when I got home at midnight, after preparing for today's hearing, my wife told me that my own 12-year-old son had asked how long it would take for his father to prove his honesty..."

The Senate committee investigating this fraud was nearing their conclusion—and closing in on indictments—when JFK was assassinated, and the new President Lyndon Johnson immediately forced the committee to disband.[45]

Perhaps Johnson got wind of what Kennedy told his private secretary, Evelyn Lincoln, on November 19, 1963. Kennedy told her he was going to drop LBJ from the 1964 ticket because of this emerging scandal and that he felt LBJ was not fit to be president. He even had a replacement picked out, Terry Sanford.[46] Sanford was an Eagle Scout, fellow World War II veteran, and the popular Democratic Governor of North Carolina. He was an early supporter of JFK's election campaign in 1960.[47] Sanford was a man of honor he could trust, and who could perhaps swing the 13 electoral votes of North Carolina, a key southern state, in 1964.[48]

The final connection to the JFK assassination is through a shady figure named Malcolm Wallace. This man was a known associate, advisor, and friend of Lyndon Johnson from his days in Texas politics in the 1950s. He was introduced to Johnson by Ed Clark, who was Johnson's lawyer. Wallace was convicted of killing miniature golf course owner John Kinser in October 1951. Kinser was having an affair with Johnson's sister, Josefa.

Wallace was convicted, but the judge suspended the sentence after pressure from Johnson.[49] This also from Marrs:

> This was not the only murder attributed to Wallace...[Another] was the death of Henry Marshall, the agriculture secretary looking into illegalities by Texas cotton allotment kingpin Billie Sol Estes...[I]n August 1984 when hearing Billie Sol Estes relate that he was present when Johnson, Wallace, and Johnson aide Cliff Carter plotted to "get rid" of Marshall...a grand jury changed the Marshall suicide ruling to one of homicide.[50]

John Harrison, a Dallas Police reservist, was inside the Texas School Book Depository within minutes of the assassination. He found evidence in the National Archives that there were over 20 fingerprints recovered from the sixth floor that could not be connected to investigators, Oswald, or employees. He took one set and gave it to Nathan Darby, a retired director of the Austin Police Department's ID and Criminal Records Section. Darby was given a jail card with Malcolm Wallace's fingerprints, and the set found in the National Archives.[51] He found a 34-point match between the two sets. In an interview in *The Men Who Killed Kennedy*, episode "The Guilty Men," Darby said: "It's a match. The finger that made the ink print also made the latent. We call that a match identified. There's no question about it. They matched. The ink in the latent print was made by the same finger. The evidence that I was presented with was Malcolm Wallace's left little finger. Without a reasonable doubt."

According to Walter Brown, a JFK assassination expert, the print came from a carboard box in the Texas School Book Depository. Fingerprints do not last long on cardboard, so it must have been placed there on November 22, 1963. "I've had too much experience. I know what I am talking about. There is no question. If I was to drop dead right now, my dying declaration," said Darby, "they match."[52] According to Marrs, "these results were made public at a news conference in May 1998, where it was announced there was no doubt that Wallace was one of the shooters."[53]

On January 7, 1971, Malcolm Wallace died suspiciously in a single car accident. There were no witnesses to the accident.[54] The accident happened three-and-a-half miles south of Pittsburg, Texas, on Route 271. The investigating officer in his report noted that the road was neither icy nor wet, but still Wallace crashed his car into an abutment, and died on impact.[55]

The situation suggested here would be without parallel in American history. The only historical example where a vice president may have been suspected of plotting to kill the commander-in-chief involves Vice President Millard Fillmore and President Zachary Taylor. In the months leading up to Taylor's death on July 9, 1850,[56] Fillmore was openly talking about measures to placate the southern states by allowing for the extension of slavery, something Taylor was against. Fillmore, a northern Whig, openly spoke of compromise with the South, so when Taylor suddenly died under perhaps suspicious circumstances, more than a few may have thought Fillmore was involved.[57] Nothing ever came of this, but when a president dies in office, the person who benefits the most is the vice president. Therefore, it seems logical to at least look that way for potential culpability.

With no love lost between Attorney General Robert Kennedy and LBJ, I do not think it would take too long for RFK to link that fingerprint to Malcolm Wallace, Johnson's henchman. That print would not get lost in the National Archives for years. So a decision would have to be made about whether to form a grand jury to indict the vice president. This would be a momentous decision. The attorney general might call Madeline Brown to testify under oath. Ed Clark, Malcolm Wallace, and Billie Sol

Estes would be charged with conspiracy as well. They might end up dying under suspicious circumstances, or be offered plea deals in exchange for testimony. If this information came out, there also might be an impeachment trial in the Senate to remove the vice president.

It might have taken years, but I envision Robert Kennedy not resting until every single person involved in this conspiracy was brought to justice. This would have meant a whole new world for the CIA and Lyndon Johnson if Clint Hill had just started running after the first shot.

Another area of change that came to an end on November 22, 1963, was the planned withdrawal of US troops from Vietnam. JFK put forth a plan to end the war by 1965. The Secretary of Defense Conference in May 1963, and another meeting of key Kennedy advisors in Hawaii in November 1963, both endorsed and recommended a phased "Vietnamization" withdrawal from Vietnam by 1965.[58] The president signed National Security Action Memorandum 263 to this effect on October 11, 1963, pledging to bring home the first 1000 advisors out of the meager total of 16,000 by December 1963, and the remainder by 1965.[59] An end to the Vietnam War in 1965 would have spared a generation of Americans the suffering that accompanied that war.

The *Encyclopedia Britannica* has the staggering figures for both Asians and Americans:

In 1995 Vietnam released its official estimate of the number of people killed during the Vietnam War: as many as 2,000,000 civilians on both sides and some 1,100,000 North Vietnamese and Viet Cong fighters. The U.S. military has estimated that between 200,000 and 250,000 South Vietnamese soldiers died. The Vietnam Veterans Memorial in Washington, D.C., lists more than 58,300 names of members of the U.S. armed forces who were killed or went missing in action. Among other countries that fought for South Vietnam, South Korea had more than 4,000 dead, Thailand about 350, Australia more than 500, and New Zealand some three dozen.[60]

All of these people would have had a chance to live their lives and enjoy a world without war in Vietnam, a war that devastated families and the environment for decades. None of that devastation would have happened if JFK had lived through his second term. There is also an equally shocking number of Vietnam War veterans who have committed suicide or fallen victim to drug addiction that could have been spared such tragedies. In Chuck Dean's book *Nam Vet*, he asserts that 150,000 Vietnam veterans have committed suicide since the war ended in 1975. He also found that the rate of divorce for Vietnam veterans is over 90 percent. Also, 500,000 veterans have been arrested, or served jail time.[61] In the book *Suicide Wall*, author Alexander Paul interviewed a Veterans' Administration (VA) doctor who said that,

> the number of Vietnam veteran suicides was 200,000 men, and that the reason the official suicide statistics were so much lower was that in many cases the suicides were documented as accidents, primarily single-car drunk driving accidents and self-inflicted gunshot wounds that were not accompanied by a suicide note...The under reporting of suicides was primarily an act of kindness to the surviving relatives.[62]

Drug addiction is also prevalent among these war veterans. Heroin addiction has led to many suicides. Heroin was first offered to these soldiers courtesy of the CIA. In 1973, Dr Lee Robins did a study of Vietnam War soldiers and discovered that almost half of them had used heroin or opium at least once during their time in Vietnam. The study said that when returning home, "rather than giving up drugs altogether, many had shifted from heroin to amphetamines or barbiturates..."[63]

The Vietnam War was also a staggering financial debacle for the United States. How much money did the United States waste, losing the Vietnam War? On June 29, 2010, the Congressional Research Service (CRS) published a study called *Cost of Major U.S. Wars*, written by Stephen Daggett, Specialist in Defense Policy and Budgets. This CRS report provides estimates of the costs of major US wars, from the American Revolution to current conflicts in Iraq, Afghanistan, and elsewhere. It presents figures both in "current year dollars," that is, in prices in effect at the time of each war, and in inflation-adjusted "constant dollars" updated to the most recently available estimates of prices in financial year 2011. All estimates are of the costs of military operations only, and do not include costs of veterans' benefits, interest paid for borrowing money to finance wars, or assistance to allies. The report also provides estimates of the cost of each war as a share of Gross Domestic Product (GDP) during the peak year of each conflict and of overall defense spending as a share of GDP at the peak.[64]

The final cost of the Vietnam War was $849 billion.[65] This number only includes the years 1965–1975,[66] not the years before, when the US was beginning occupation. It also does not include those factors Daggett left out, meaning the figure is likely $1 trillion. The United States population in 1975 was 219,081,250 people.[67] That means an average family of four people would have spent about $18,256 on losing that war. According to the inflation calculator, $18,256 in 1975 is $100,547.46 in 2022.[68] A $1 trillion investment in the economy could have ended child poverty, among many other things.

With President Kennedy moving through his second term with a dismantled CIA, the agency would be unable to continue its illegal drug trafficking in Laos and South America. The president worked against the agency for years to stop this, all the way up until the month of his assassination. The entire story is in my book *Why the CIA Killed JFK and Malcolm X: The Secret Drug Trade in Laos*. If he was able to stop this illegal drug trafficking, the opiates epidemic that has spread through the US and South America possibly could have been avoided.

Two other accomplishments that were JFK's ideas but happened in subsequent administrations would have ended up taking place in his administration instead. These would be the passage of the Civil Rights Act, and the moon landing. JFK proposed the passage of the Civil Rights Act in a speech to the nation on June 11, 1963.[69] The Civil Rights Act was signed into law by Lyndon Johnson on July 2, 1964.[70] Kennedy proposed landing a man on the moon and returning him safely to the earth by the end of the decade in a speech at Rice University on September 12, 1962.[71] The moon landing eventually took place on July 20, 1969, under the administration of Richard Nixon.[72]

There is a good chance, though, that the president would have wanted to push up the timetables for these things if possible before he left office in January 1969. The reason may shock some people, but one of JFK's ideas for how to end the Cold War was to stage a joint Soviet–American moon landing. Apparently, the Soviets were prepared to accept the offer. *Space Cast News Service* in an October 7, 1997, report provided the details behind what would have been a world-changing event:

Soviet Premiere Nikita S. Khrushchev reversed himself in early November, 1963, and had at the time, decided to accept U.S. President John F. Kennedy's offer to convert the Apollo lunar landing program into a joint project to explore the Moon with Soviet and U.S. astronauts, SpaceCast learned Wednesday from one of the last remaining participants in the decision still alive.

On the eve of the 40th anniversary of the world's first space satellite, the Soviet Sputnik 1, Sergei Khrushchev, eldest son of the former Premiere and Soviet Union Communist Party General Secretary said that his father made the decision in November 1963 following a renewed Kennedy initiative to sell the Soviets on a joint manned lunar program.

"My father decided that maybe he should accept (Kennedy's) offer, given the state of the space programs of the two countries (in 1963)," Khrushchev told SpaceCast following a talk before a NASA conference in Washington on the effects of the historic Sputnik launch on Oct. 4, 1957...

Kennedy had made the offer of a joint manned lunar program to the Russians on several occasions, but his most aggressive effort was made in a speech before the United Nations General Assembly on Sept. 20, 1963, in New York.

At the end of that address, Kennedy said: "In a field where the United States and the Soviet Union have a special capacity—space—there is room for new cooperation, for further joint efforts."

"I include among these possibilities," he added, "a joint expedition to the Moon." Why, the President asked, should the United States and the Soviet Union conduct parallel efforts that would include "duplication, of research, construction, and expenditure?"

He laid out a proposal for a joint series of space missions, which if enacted, he said "will require a new approach to the Cold War."...

[T]he prospects of a visit to the Soviet Union by President Kennedy during the 1964 Presidential campaign, suggested by several former Kennedy administration staffers, or a visit to Russia early in a Kennedy second term, might well have cemented the joint lunar plan. And such a Kennedy/ Khrushchev initiative might have staved off the planning of a coup that eventually removed Khrushchev from office in October, 1964.

"I think," Sergei Khrushchev said, "if Kennedy had lived, we would be living in a completely different world." But a week after the reversal decision was allegedly made, Kennedy was assassinated in Dallas, Texas and the decision was dropped.[73]

The dream of a joint Russian–American moon landing also died with President Kennedy.

One other thing that might have happened during the remaining time in office for JFK was another addition to the Kennedy family. On August 9, 1963, Patrick Bouvier Kennedy died after just three days in this world.[74] The death of their newborn brought the first couple closer together. I think that in 1965 they would try again to have another child, perhaps naming him Joseph Kennedy III, after JFK's father and older brother. When the time came for JFK to leave office after his second term, he would still be a young man, with much of his life ahead of him. He would turn 52 years old on May 29, 1969.[75] In the 1970s, he would have enjoyed watching his children grow up and get into politics. John F. Kennedy Jr would likely run for the Senate in New York State in the 1990s, and then run for president, perhaps in 2004. JFK may have even grown restless and taken a position on the United States Supreme Court at some point.

But perhaps most of all, the greatest benefit of him surviving the assassination would be to spare the country the collective sorrow and pain that the assassination caused. This was especially felt by his wife Jacqueline after his tragic death. The sorrow she experienced was conveyed in a letter she penned to her minister, Washington Auxiliary Bishop Philip Hannan, who delivered Kennedy's eulogy. Jacqueline Kennedy wrote to Hannan to thank him for his support in her time of need:

"I haven't believed in the child's vision of heaven for a long time. There is no way now to commune with him. It will be so long before I am dead and even then, I don't know if I will be reunited with him," she wrote on December 20, 1963. "Even if I am I don't think you could ever convince me that it will be the way it was while we were married here. Please forgive all this— and please don't try to convince me just yet—I shouldn't be writing this way."[76] Mrs. Kennedy then summed up the feelings of the entire nation in the next sentence. "If only I could believe that he could look down and see how he is missed, and how nobody will ever be the same without him."[77]

If President Kennedy had survived his assassination, here is what I envision his final years would have looked like. Future President Bill Clinton met President Kennedy on July 24, 1963, in the White House Rose Garden. Clinton, who was 16 years old at the time, had been selected as one of two members of Arkansas' delegation for Boys' Nation, organized by the American Legion.[78] When he became president, Clinton appointed JFK's sister Jean Kennedy Smith to be ambassador to Ireland in 1993.[79] I could easily see Clinton instead offering this position to the former president, Clinton's boyhood hero, as a way for JFK to spend his later years in the Kennedy family's ancestral land.

Three months into his presidency, President Clinton would appoint JFK to be ambassador to Ireland, on May 29, 1993, Kennedy's 76th birthday.[80] JFK would likely stay on until Clinton left office in January 2001. JFK would then return home to the Kennedy compound in Hyannis Port, Massachusetts, likely dying within a few years, perhaps after his 86th birthday. It would be November 2003, and the Kennedy compound would be preparing for two special birthdays. JFK Jr was turning 43 on November 25.[81] This was the same age as his father was when he ran for president in 1960. JFK Jr had a big announcement. He was going to run for president in 2004. Caroline Kennedy, JFK's daughter, was turning 46 on November 27.[82] She would be her brother's campaign manager.

The idea was to celebrate and make the announcement the weekend before the birthdays, but the former president was in failing health. The family arrived on Friday, November 21, 2003.[83] Robert Kennedy and his children came, and Ted Kennedy was there as well. During the night, the former president contracted a fever, and a doctor was called in. The following day his conditioned worsened and it was clear the president was in his final hours. The old war hero would be surrounded by his loving family, his brothers Robert and Teddy, his grandchildren near his bed, waiting for the end. Then the time would come, the good work finally over, and a grateful nation would mourn his loss. The date was November 22, 2003.

Endnotes

Chapter 1

1   http://www.encyclopediaofalabama.org/article/m-3598
2   https://www.newyorkalmanack.com/2019/12/1861-lincoln-and-john-wilkes-booth-in-albany/
3   https://www.womenhistoryblog.com/2013/09/clara-harris-rathbone.html
4   Ibid.
5   Ibid.
6   Ibid.
7   Ibid.
8   http://alloveralbany.com/archive/2015/02/18/the-time-lincoln-and-booth-crossed-paths-in-albany
9   https://www.newyorkalmanack.com/2019/12/1861-lincoln-and-john-wilkes-booth-in-albany/
10 Ibid.
11 Ibid.
12 https://spectrumlocalnews.com/nys/buffalo/albany-archives/2016/02/15/albany-archives-lincoln-and-john-wilkes-boothe-four-years-before-assassination
13 https://www.history.com/this-day-in-history/robert-e-lee-surrenders
14 http://www.abrahamlincolnonline.org/lincoln/speeches/last.htm
15 https://historynewsnetwork.org/article/175394
16 William Tidwell, et al., *Come Retribution: The Confederate Secret Service and the Assassination of Lincoln* (New York, NY: Barnes and Noble Books, 1988), 24.
17 All examples cited from ibid., 5–6.
18 Ibid., 18.
19 Ibid., 5.

20 Ibid., 21.
21 Ibid., 26.
22 Ibid., 27.
23 Ibid., 28–9.

Chapter 2

1 https://www.fords.org/lincolns-assassination/booths-deringer/

2 https://www.nationalparks.org/connect/blog/gun-shot-lincoln

3 https://www.pewpewtactical.com/guns-used-in-assassinations/

4 https://www.deseret.com/1994/6/1/19112083/caption-only-booth-gun-fetches-70-000#:~:text=Booth%20gun%20fetches%20%2470%2C000%20A,day%20after%20Lincoln%20was%20shot.

5 https://www.ripleys.com/weird-news/could-this-be-the-derringer-responsible-for-abraham-lincolns-demise/

6 Ibid.

7 Author visit to Ford's Theater, November 12, 2022.

8 https://twitter.com/LinConspirators/status/1438104596384260102/photo/2

9 https://www.washingtonpost.com/blogs/political-bookworm/post/oreilly-book-banned-from-fords-theatre/2011/11/12/gIQAEzvOGN_blog.html. His name was incorrectly listed as James J. Clifford in inaccurate renderings of the assassination.

10 https://rogerjnorton.com/LincolnDiscussionSymposium/post-62776.html

11 https://babel.hathitrust.org/cgi/pt?id=uiug.30112004527377&view=1up&seq=362&q1= plowman

12 https://idnc.library.illinois. edu/?a=d&d=NYC19110902.2.132&e=-------en-20--1--img-txIN

13 https://www.inquirer.com/philly/news/20130820_Booth_
killed_Lincoln_with_a_pistol_made_in_Northern_
Liberties.html

14 https://idnc.library.illinois.edu/?a=d&d=NYC19110902.2.132&
e=-------en-20--1--img-txIN

15 https://hsp.org/blogs/question-of-the-week/john-wilkes-
booth-joined-which-philadelphia-theatre-company-
in-1857

16 https://www.wondersandmarvels.com/2010/12/five-
surprising-facts-about-the-booth-brothers.html

17 Michael W. Kauffman, *American Brutus: John Wilkes Booth
and the Lincoln Conspiracies* (New York, NY: Random House,
2004), 103.

18 https://idnc.library.illinois.edu/?a=d&d=NYC19110902.2.
132&e=-------en-20--1--img-txIN

19 https://books.google.com/books?id=pm6bgyVbzxgC&pg=
RA1-PA1882#v=onepage&q&f=false

20 Email, Tacita Barrera, August 25, 2022.

21 https://archives.fbi.gov/archives/news/stories/2004/march/
lincoln_031804

22 Email, Tacita Barrera, August 26, 2022.

Chapter 3

1 https://digitalcommons.lasalle.edu/philadelphia_civil_
war_2/14/

2 https://www.history.com/news/john-wilkes-booth-family

3 History of the Theatre – Walnut Street Theatre –
Philadelphia, PA – Official Website

4 Ibid.

5 Michael W. Kauffman, *American Brutus: John Wilkes Booth
and the Lincoln Conspiracies* (New York, NY: Random House,
2004), 117.

6 Ibid., 97.

7   Ibid., 98.

8   Ibid., 99.

9   https://www.nps.gov/articles/000/south-carolina-secession.htm

10   Kauffman, 111.

11   Ibid., 112.

12   Ibid., 142.

13   Ibid., 160.

14   https://www.loc.gov/resource/highsm.04710/?r=0.3,0.353,0.261,0.106,0

15   https://m.facebook.com/PhiladelphiaStoriesbyBobMcNulty/photos/john-wilkes-booth-assassinated-president-abraham-lincoln-at-fords-theatre-in-was/1436764569828462/

16   Ibid.

17   William Tidwell, et al., *Come Retribution: The Confederate Secret Service and the Assassination of Lincoln* (New York, NY: Barnes and Noble Books, 1988), 403.

18   Ibid., 404.

19   https://digitalcommons.lasalle.edu/philadelphia_civil_war_2/14/

20   Tidwell, 405.

21   Kauffman, 212.

22   https://www.britannica.com/biography/Abraham-Lincoln

23   McElroy Philadelphia 1865 City Directory, 860.

24   Ibid.

25   https://www.bing.com/maps?q=map%20of%20philadelphia&qs=n&form=QBRE&=Search%20%7B0%7D%20for%20%7B1%7D&=Search%20work%20for%20%7B0%7D&=%25eManage%20Your%20Search%20History%25E&sp=-1&pq=map%20of%20philadelphia&sc=6-19&sk=&

26   https://www.bing.com/maps?q=map%20of%20philadelphia&qs=n&form=QBRE&=Search%20%7B0%7D%20for%20%7B1%7D&=Search%20work%20for%20%20

%7B0%7D&=%25eManage%20Your%20Search%20History%25E&sp=-1&pq=map%20of%20philadelphia&sc=6-19&sk=&cvid=903F841249B949709E7110030D1ADFB0&ghsh=0&ghacc=0&ghpl=cvid=903F841249B949709E7110030D1ADFB0&ghsh=0&ghacc=0&ghpl=

27 McElroy Philadelphia 1865 City Directory, 860.

28 William Afferbach, 1141 N 2nd; Jesse Butterfield, 1528 Frankford Ave; De Binder, 120 South; Joseph Grugg, 236 Market; John Krider, NE 2nd and Walnut; Francis Lins, 116 Girard; Frederick Lins, S51 and 2nd; Richardson and Overman, SE 11th and Thompson; Samuel Spang, 148 N 3rd; Tyron E. and K., 625 Market, 616 Commerce, and 229 N 2nd; Tyson and Bro., 220 N 3rd.

Chapter 4

1 https://www.smithsonianmag.com/history/lincolns-missing-bodyguard-12932069/

2 Ibid.

3 https://www.womenhistoryblog.com/2013/09/clara-harris-rathbone.html

4 Ibid.

5 Ibid.

6 https://www.thoughtco.com/civil-rights-act-of-1866-4164345

7 Ibid.

8 https://www.history.com/topics/black-history/freedmens-bureau#section_1

9 Ibid.

10 Ibid.

11 Ibid.

12 https://www.history.com/this-day-in-history/president-andrew-johnson-impeached

13 http://www.abrahamlincolnonline.org/lincoln/speeches/last.htm

14 https://ameicainpalestine.blogspot.com/2013/09/america-and-jews-of-palestine.html

15 https://allthatsinteresting.com/mary-todd-lincoln

Chapter 5

1 Carter Smith, *Presidents: All You Need to Know* (Irvington, NY: Hylas, 2004), 130.

2 David M. Jordan, *Roscoe Conkling of New York: A Voice in the Senate* (Ithaca, NY: Cornell University Press, 1971), 337.

3 Ibid., 351.

4 Ibid.

5 Ibid., 353.

6 Ibid.

7 Ibid., 357.

8 James C. Clark, *The Murder of James A. Garfield: The President's Last Days and the Trial and Execution of His Assassin* (Jefferson, NC: McFarland and Co., 1993), 34.

9 Jordan, 369.

10 Ibid., 370.

11 Ibid., 381.

12 Clark, 40.

13 Smith, 133.

14 Jordan, 387.

15 Smith, 133.

Chapter 6

1 http://www.powerfulwords.info/speeches/presidential-speeches/presidential-speech-james-abram-garfield.html

2 Ibid.

3 Ibid.

4 Ibid.

5 James C. Clark, *The Murder of James A. Garfield: The President's Last Days and the Trial and Execution of His Assassin* (Jefferson, NC: McFarland and Co., 1993), 16.

6   https://www.history.com/news/the-assassination-of-president-james-a-garfield

7   Ibid.

Chapter 7

1   https://ohiohistorycentral.org/w/Murat_Halstead

2   https://www.goodreads.com/author/list/230666.Murat_Halstead

3   Murat Halstead, *The Illustrious Life of William McKinley, Our Martyred President* (1901), 72.

4   James C. Clark, *The Murder of James A. Garfield: The President's Last Days and the Trial and Execution of His Assassin* (Jefferson, NC: McFarland and Co., 1993), 51.

5   Halstead, 72.

6   Ibid.

7   Ibid., 73.

8   https://www.whitehousehistory.org/press-room/press-timelines/guarding-the-white-house

9   https://www.whitehousehistory.org/photos/thomas-f-pendel-a-white-house-doorman-for-thirty-six-years

10 Halstead, 73.

11 Clark, 51.

12 Ibid., 56.

13 Ibid.

14 https://millercenter.org/president/garfield/essays/hunt-1881-william-secretary-of-the-navy

15 https://millercenter.org/president/garfield/essays/windom-william-1881-secretary-of-the-treasury

16 https://www.secretservice.gov/about/history/timeline

17 Clark, 61.

18 https://www.britannica.com/biography/Cyrus-W-Field

19 https://www.facebook.com/GarfieldNPS/posts/1390902474297661

20   Clark, 57.

21   Ibid., 64–5.

22   Garfield Criminal Case File, 14065, Library of Congress. Research days: February 19, February 20, 2015.

23   https://www.archives.gov/publications/prologue/2008/ spring/metro-police.html#nt21

Chapter 8

1   James C. Clark, *The Murder of James A. Garfield: The President's Last Days and the Trial and Execution of His Assassin* (Jefferson, NC: McFarland and Co., 1993), 54.

2   Ibid., 53.

3   https://www.battlefields.org/learn/revolutionary-war/ battles/yorktown

4   https://www.battlefields.org/learn/civil-war/battles/ atlanta

5   https://www.nps.gov/articles/000/james-a-garfield-and-the-civil-war-part-ii.htm

6   Ibid.

7   Ibid.

8   https://millercenter.org/president/garfield/essays/ macveagh-isaac-wayne-1881-attorney-general

9   https://www.smithsonianmag.com/history/created-150-years-ago-justice-departments-first-mission-was-protect-black-rights-180975232/

10   https://www.nga.org/governor/samuel-jordan-kirkwood/

11   Ibid.

12   http://werehistory.org/garfield-2/

13   Clark, 37.

14   https://www.270towin.com/1884_Election/

15   https://www.archives.gov/milestone-documents/ pendleton-act

16   Clark, 41.

17   Ibid.

18   https://www2.tompkinscountyny.gov/files2/personnel/
     CIVIL%20SERVICE%20IN%20NEW%20YORK%20STATE%20
     HISTORY%20AND%20OVERVIEW%20-%20revised%20
     5.19.2020.pdf

19   https://www.u-s-history.com/pages/h738.html

20   Ibid.

21   https://ballotpedia.org/Federal_judges_nominated_by_
     Chester_Arthur

22   https://ballotpedia.org/Federal_judges_nominated_by_
     Grover_Cleveland

23   http://www.zinnedproject.org/news/tdih/wilmington-
     massacre-2/

Chapter 9

1   James C. Clark, *The Murder of James A. Garfield: The President's
    Last Days and the Trial and Execution of His Assassin* (Jefferson,
    NC: McFarland and Co., 1993), 54.

2   https://www.guns.com/news/2013/04/22/british-bulldog-
    pocket-revolvers

3   Clark, 48–9.

4   Boyd's 1881 City Directory District of Columbia.

5   https://www.google.com/maps/search/washington+dc+us
    +treasury/@38.8976337,-77.0337571,19.25z

6   https://www.google.com/maps/dir/Washington+DC+Eco
    nomic+Partnership,+F+Street+Northwest,+Washington,+D
    C/1413+G+St+NW,+Washington,+DC+20005/@38.897969,-
    77.035069,17z/data=!3m1!4b1!4m13!4m12!1m5!1m1!1s0x89b
    7b7bd622a12ab:0xf3a13593d27505f6!2m2!1d-77.0332432!2d3
    8.8976301!1m5!1m1!1s0x89b7b796329f78b9:0x77d4bb09
    db2c1c05!2m2!1d-77.0327023!2d38.8985781 Author visit to
    Washington DC, November 12, 2022.

Chapter 10

1   James C. Clark, *The Murder of James A. Garfield: The President's Last Days and the Trial and Execution of His Assassin* (Jefferson, NC: McFarland and Co., 1993), 58.

2   Ibid.

3   Ibid.

4   Ibid., 60.

5   https://archive.org/details/boydsdirectoryof1881wash/page/816/mode/2up?q=+page+816&view=theater

6   *Washington Post*, July 3, 1881 https://www.loc.gov/resource/mss21956.mss21956-177_0370_0514/?sp=3&r=0.472,0.08,0.453,0.186,0

7   Clark, 56.

8   https://archive.org/details/boydsdirectoryof1881wash/page/816/mode/2up?q=+page+816&view=theater and https://www.loc.gov/resource/mss21956.mss21956-177_0370_0514/?sp=13&r=0.485,0.379,0.417,0.171,0

9   https://rogerjnorton.com/LincolnDiscussionSymposium/thread-2197-post-43976.html#pid43976

10   https://www.loc.gov/resource/mss21956.mss21956-177_0370_0514/?sp=13&r=0.485,0.379,0.417,0.171,0

11   https://www.dccourts.gov/historic-commemoration

12   Clark, 121.

13   Ibid., 139.

14   Ibid.

15   https://www.historicalfirearms.info/post/45532878814/the-gun-that-killed-us-president-james-garfield

16   Clark, 49.

17   https://images.findagrave.com/photos/2021/305/150753587_c8ae5e73-5a22-4c60-9e8d-abc8f7095b5e.jpeg

18   https://www.archives.gov/files/research/district-of-columbia/police-force-1861-1968.pdf

19   https://www.theatlantic.com/politics/archive/2015/10/this-is-the-brain-that-shot-president-james-garfield/454212/

20 *Washington Post*, July 10, 1881.

Part III
1   https://www.buffaloah.com/a/niagSq/mck/index.html

Chapter 11
1   https://www.trsite.org/learn/the-pan-american-expo
2   https://www.buffaloah.com/h/mckinley.html Canisius High School owns the land now.
3   A. Wesley Johns, *The Man Who Shot McKinley: A New View of the Assassination of the President* (Cranbury, NJ: A.S. Barnes and Co., 1970), 30.
4   Ibid., 39.
5   Ibid.
6   https://www.shapell.org/manuscript/president-mckinley-first-lady-fall-ill-in-san-francisco
7   Johns, 136.
8   Ibid., 30.
9   Ibid.
10 Jack C. Fisher, *Stolen Glory: The McKinley Assassination* (La Jolla, CA: Alamar Books, 2001), 46, 223 note 6.
11 Johns, 136.
12 Eric Rauchway, *Murdering McKinley: The Making of Theodore Roosevelt's America* (New York, NY: Hill and Wang, 2003), 177.
13 Murat Halstead, *The Illustrious Life of William McKinley, Our Martyred President* (1901), 90.
14 G.W. Townsend, *Memorial Life of William McKinley, Our Martyred President* (Memorial Publishing Co., 1901), 222.
15 Halstead, 90.
16 "Officer Ireland Tells His Story of the Shooting, He Declares It Was Done So Quickly There Was No Time to Do Anything," *Buffalo Evening News*, September 7, 1901.
17 Halstead, 68.

18 Johns, 218.
19 Ibid., 193.
20 Townsend, 248.
21 Ibid., 75.
22 Thomas Leary and Elizabeth Sholes, *Buffalo's Pan-American Exposition* (Charleston, SC: Arcadia, 1998).
23 Jeffrey W. Seibert, *I Done My Duty: The Complete Story of the Assassination of President McKinley* (Bowie, MD: Heritage Books, 2002), 47.
24 https://digital.lib.buffalo.edu/items/show/91878
25 Seibert, 47.
26 John Koerner, *The Secret Plot to Kill McKinley* (Western New York Wares, 2011), 44. The photograph in question is on page 44.

Chapter 12

1 https://www.pbs.org/newshour/health/would-mckinley-have-survived-an-assassins-bullet-if-he-had-a-different-doctor
2 https://www.tribtoday.com/news/local-news/2021/06/mckinley-quells-rumors-that-hell-run-for-a-third-term/
3 https://shapell.org/manuscript/president-mckinley-first-lady-fall-ill-in-san-francisco/
4 https://firstladies.org/biographies/firstladies.aspx?biography=25
5 https://avalon.law.yale.edu/19th_century/mckin2.asp
6 https://www.270towin.com/1904_Election/
7 https://www.britannica.com/biography/Theodore-Roosevelt
8 https://www.270towin.com/1912_Election/
9 https://www.nobelprize.org/prizes/peace/1906/roosevelt/facts/
10 https://www.britannica.com/biography/Theodore-Roosevelt

Chapter 13

1 Jack C. Fisher, *Stolen Glory: The McKinley Assassination* (La Jolla, CA: Alamar Books, 2001), 45.

2 A. Wesley Johns, *The Man Who Shot McKinley* (Cranbury, NJ: A.S. Barnes and Co., 1970), 49.

3 Fisher, 46.

4 Buffalo City Directory, 1901, 38.

5 Email, Wayne Mori, July 3, 2022,

6 *Buffalo Courier*, June 9, 1900.

7 Ibid.

8 Buffalo City Directory, 1901, 102.

9 https://deadmalls.com/malls/main_place_mall.html

10 Fisher, 46.

11 Ibid.

12 Ibid., 159.

13 Ibid., 46.

14 https://www.guns.com/news/2013/04/20/iver-johnson-safety-revolvers-glorious-contradictions

15 Fisher, 222.

16 Fisher, 159.

Chapter 14

1 https://buffalohistory.pastperfectonline.com/webobject/94CBB9DC-1A2C-4DF9-9071-768718222846

2 Jack C. Fisher, *Stolen Glory: The McKinley Assassination* (La Jolla, CA: Alamar Books, 2001), 60.

3 Email, Walter Mayer, July 15, 2022. Words in square brackets are the author's.

4 https://www.roadsideamerica.com/blog/mckinleys-gun/

Chapter 15

1 Jim Marrs, *Crossfire: The Plot That Killed Kennedy*, revised and updated (New York, NY: Basic Books, 2013), 344.

2   https://www.youtube.com/watch?v=5p4AvezLnG0
3   https://www.odmp.org/officer/13338-officer-j-d-tippit
4   https://texashistory.unt.edu/ark:/67531/metapth190306/ m1/15/
5   Marrs, 415.
6   Ibid.
7   Ibid.
8   Robert J. Groden, *The Killing of a President* (New York, NY: Viking Studio Books, 1993), 86–7.
9   https://www.youtube.com/watch?v=lQ435lMaCng
10 https://www.merriam-webster.com/dictionary/paraffin%20 test
11 https://www.youtube.com/watch?v=LvgT4rvQH1g
12 Marrs, 421.
13 Ibid., 422.
14 Ibid.
15 Ibid., 423.
16 Ibid.
17 Ibid., 423–4.
18 Ibid., 191.
19 Ibid., 418.
20 Ibid.
21 Ibid.
22 Groden, 66, 176.
23 Ibid.
24 Ibid.
25 Marrs, 420.
26 Ibid., 419.
27 Ibid.
28 Ibid., 421.
29 Ibid., 50–1.
30 Ibid., 52.
31 https://www.youtube.com/watch?v=ve4AcZZBPkc
32 http://harveyandlee.net/No_Stairs/No_Stairs.html

Chapter 16

1 https://www.recoilweb.com/carcano-kennedy-assassination-rifle-161186.html

2 Robert J. Groden, *The Killing of a President* (New York, NY: Viking Studio Books, 1993), 103.

3 Jim Marrs, *Crossfire: The Plot That Killed Kennedy*, revised and updated (New York, NY: Basic Books, 2013), 419.

4 Marrs, 420.

5 Ibid.

6 Ibid., 421.

7 https://www.archives.gov/research/jfk/faqs#rifle

8 https://catalog.archives.gov/id/305134

9 Ibid.

10 Ibid.

Chapter 17

1 Robert J. Groden, *The Killing of a President* (New York, NY: Viking Studio Books, 1993), 20.

2 https://foreignpolicy.com/2017/05/22/may-20-1937-orwell-is-shot-in-the-neck/

3 Groden, 20–8.

4 https://www.youtube.com/watch?v=ve4AcZZBPkc

5 https://www.youtube.com/watch?v=q-vmn5eAEAw "Examining the Zapruder Film Fakery."

6 Groden, 41.

7 https://www.irishcentral.com/roots/history/did-irish-william-greer-cause-jfks-death

8 https://jfkwitnesses.omeka.net/exhibits/show/secret/odonnell

9 https://www.irishcentral.com/roots/history/did-irish-william-greer-cause-jfks-death and Jim Marrs, *Crossfire: The Plot That Killed Kennedy*, revised and updated (New York, NY: Basic Books, 2013), 232.

10 Marrs, 229–30.

11 https://www.vanityfair.com/news/politics/2014/10/secret-service-jfk-assassination
12 Ibid.
13 Ibid.
14 Ibid.
15 Ibid.
16 https://www.blackpast.org/african-american-history/bolden-abraham-1935/
17 https://www.washingtoninformer.com/black-secret-service-agent-under-jfk-pardoned-by-president-joe-biden/

Chapter 18
1   https://millercenter.org/the-presidency/presidential-speeches/august-27-1964-acceptance-speech-democratic-national
2   https://www.pewresearch.org/fact-tank/2019/07/05/jfks-america/
3   http://content.time.com/time/specials/2007/article/0,28804,1635958_1635999_1634964,00.html
4   http://www.peacecorps.gov/about/history/
5   http://www.bibliotecapleyades.net/sociopolitica/esp_sociopol_secretgov_5i.htm
6   http://www.jfklibrary.org/Asset-Viewer/Archives/JFKPOF-TPH-17B-1.aspx. The full recording can be heard here.
7   http://ratical.org/ratville/JFK/Unspeakable/Item03.pdf
8   http://www.bibliotecapleyades.net/sociopolitica/esp_sociopol_secretgov_5i.htm
9   http://www.peacecorps.gov/about/jobs/workingpc/eligibility/
10 http://www.ratical.org/ratville/JFK/USO/appE.html NSAM 56 incidentally was simply an inventory, a review of paramilitary operations ordered by National Security Advisor McGeorge Bundy.

11 Ibid.

12 https://publicintelligence.net/operation-northwoods/

13 https://www.britannica.com/biography/E-Howard-Hunt

14 "The Last Confession of E. Howard Hunt," *Rolling Stone*, April 5, 2007.

15 https://www.youtube.com/watch?v=q-vmn5eAEAw "Examining the Zapruder Film Fakery."

16 https://www.youtube.com/watch?v=OGr21FZBVL4 and https://vimeo.com/ondemand/killingoswald/102327635

17 Jim Marrs, *Crossfire: The Plot That Killed Kennedy*, revised and updated (New York, NY: Basic Books, 2013), 191.

18 https://www.merriam-webster.com/dictionary/treason

19 https://constitutionus.com/democracy/treason-and-the-us-constitution/

20 "CIA: Marker of Policy or Tool? Survey finds widely feared agency is tightly controlled," *New York Times*, April 25, 1966.

21 Karl Evanzz, *The Judas Factor: The Plot to Kill Malcolm X* (New York, NY: Thunder's Mouth Press, 1992), 76, 318.

22 Ibid., 294.

23 James W. Douglass, "The Murder and Martyrdom of Malcolm," in James DiEugenio and Lisa Pease (eds), *The Assassinations: Probe Magazine on JFK, MLK, RFK and Malcolm X* (Los Angeles, CA: Feral House, 2003), 409.

24 Evanzz, 255.

25 Ibid.

26 Ibid.

27 Ibid., 256.

28 Ibid.

29 Miriam Sagan, *Mysterious Deaths: Malcolm X* (San Diego, CA: Lucent Books, 1997), 25.

30 Ibid., 68.

31 https://m.facebook.com/StrikeMachine/photos/a.10295302 1413650/141653640876921/?type =3

32 Douglass, 404.

33 Ibid., 411.

34 https://www.bing.com/search?q=malcolm+x+assasins+set+free&cvid=3435c9f6e1084b0180 3ad9856dd64de5&aqs=ed ge69i57.8421j0j1&pglt=41&FORM=ANNTA1&PC=DCTS

35 https://www.reuters.com/legal/malcolm-xs-daughter-sue-cia-fbi-new-york-police-over-assassination-2023-02-21/

36 https://lipstick-and-war-crimes.org/hiding-the-verdict-the-1999-martin-luther-king-civil-trial/

37 https://abcnews.go.com/US/robert-kennedys-killer-sirhan-sirhan-brainwashed/story?id=13029050

38 https://www.huffpost.com/entry/rfk-assassination-nina-rhodes-hughes_n_1464439

39 https://youtu.be/NZKjm9ezTXQ "Kennedy Assassination - Lyndon Johnson Killed JFK - The Men Who Killed Kennedy."

40 Robert Bryce, *Cronies: Oil, the Bushes, and the Rise of Texas, America's Superstate* (Public Affairs, 2004).

41 https://assassinationofjfk.net/category/assassination-of-jfk/

42 https://millercenter.org/the-presidency/presidential-speeches/january-14-1963-state-union-address

43 https://youtu.be/NZKjm9ezTXQ "Kennedy Assassination - Lyndon Johnson Killed JFK - The Men Who Killed Kennedy."

44 https://youtu.be/NZKjm9ezTXQ "Kennedy Assassination - Lyndon Johnson Killed JFK - The Men Who Killed Kennedy."

45 https://lbjthemasterofdeceit.com/

46 https://educationforum.ipbhost.com/topic/15790-bobby-baker-scandal-and-the-assassination-of-jfk/ and https://www.google.com/url?sa=t&rct=j&q=&esrc=s&source=web&cd=&cad=rja&uact=8&ved=2ahUKEwi4tI-

3laL5AhXwEGIAHZ_ODZcQFnoECAQQAQ&url=https
%3A%2F%2Fwww.thedailybeast.com%2Fit-will-not-be-
lyndon-why-jfk-wanted-to-drop-lbj-for-reelection&usg=A
OvVaw048D3W1SqtY0x2HEDydq4v

47 https://northcarolinahistory.org/encyclopedia/terry-
sanford-1917-1998/
48 https://www.270towin.com/1964_Election/
49 Marrs, 294.
50 Ibid.
51 Ibid.
52 https://youtu.be/NZKjm9ezTXQ "Kennedy Assassination -
Lyndon Johnson Killed JFK - The Men Who Killed
Kennedy."
53 Marrs, 294.
54 https://youtu.be/NZKjm9ezTXQ "Kennedy Assassination -
Lyndon Johnson Killed JFK - The Men Who Killed
Kennedy."
55 https://alchetron.com/Malcolm-Wallace
56 https://www.whitehouse.gov/about-the-white-house/
presidents/millard-fillmore/
57 https://history-first.com/2018/07/10/millard-fillmore-
zachary-taylor-and-american-conspiracies/
58 http://jfkfacts.org/assassination/experts/was-jfk-going-to-
pull-out-of-vietnam/
59 National Security Action Memoranda [NSAM]: NSAM 263,
South Vietnam | JFK Library
60 https://www.britannica.com/question/How-many-people-
died-in-the-Vietnam-War
61 https://pubmed.ncbi.nlm.nih.gov/16179335/
62 Ibid.
63 http://www.suicidewall.com/suicide-statistics/
64 https://sgp.fas.org/crs/natsec/RS22926.pdf
65 Ibid.

66 Ibid.
67 https://www.bing.com/search?q=us+population+in+1975&c
    vid=b6b8ae4857bf441d82fae277 5c4cabe5&aqs=edge.0.0l9.1
    0970j0j1&pglt=2083&FORM=ANNTA1&PC=HCTS
68 https://www.usinflationcalculator.com/
69 https://www.pbs.org/wgbh/americanexperience/features/
    president-kennedy-civil-rights/
70 https://www.archives.gov/milestone-documents/civil-
    rights-act
71 https://www.rev.com/blog/transcripts/john-f-kennedy-jfk-
    moon-speech-transcript-we-choose-to-go-to-the-moon It is
    interesting that Kennedy liked to make major speeches on
    his wedding anniversary, including his Houston Ministers
    speech on September 12, 1960.
72 https://www.history.com/topics/space-exploration/moon-
    landing-1969
73 https://www.spacedaily.com/news/russia-97h.html
74 https://www.irishcentral.com/roots/history/tragic-death-
    patrick-kennedy-jfk-jackie
75 https://www.history.com/topics/us-presidents/john-f-
    kennedy
76 https://www.thedailybeast.com/kennedy-funeral-and-
    jackie-onassis-letters-by-archbisop-hannan
77 Ibid.
78 https://www.biography.com/news/john-f-kennedy-bill-
    clinton-handshake-1963
79 https://www.nbcnews.com/news/us-news/jean-kennedy-
    smith-last-surviving-sibling-president-kennedy-dies-
    92-n1231401
80 https://www.britannica.com/biography/John-F-Kennedy
81 https://www.biography.com/history-culture/john-f-
    kennedy-jr

82   https://www.biography.com/history-culture/caroline-kennedy

83   https://www.timeanddate.com/calendar/index.html?year=2003&country=1

CHRONOS
BOOKS

HISTORY

Chronos Books is an historical nonfiction imprint. Chronos
publishes real history for real people, bringing to life people,
places, and events in an imaginative, easy-to-digest and
accessible way — histories that pass on their stories to a
generation of new readers.
If you have enjoyed this book, why not tell other readers by
posting a review on your preferred book site.

Recent bestsellers from Chronos Books are:

Lady Katherine Knollys
The Unacknowledged Daughter of King Henry VIII
Sarah-Beth Watkins
A comprehensive account of Katherine Knollys' questionable
paternity, her previously unexplored life in the Tudor court
and her intriguing relationship with Elizabeth I.
Paperback: 978-1-78279-585-8 ebook: 978-1-78279-584-1

Cromwell was Framed
Ireland 1649
Tom Reilly
Revealed: The definitive research that proves the Irish nation
owes Oliver Cromwell a huge posthumous apology for
wrongly convicting him of civilian atrocities in 1649.
Paperback: 978-1-78279-516-2 ebook: 978-1-78279-515-5

Why The CIA Killed JFK and Malcolm X
The Secret Drug Trade in Laos
John Koerner
A new groundbreaking work presenting evidence that the CIA
silenced JFK to protect its secret drug trade in Laos.
Paperback: 978-1-78279-701-2 ebook: 978-1-78279-700-5

The Disappearing Ninth Legion
A Popular History
Mark Olly
The Disappearing Ninth Legion examines hard evidence
for the foundation, development, mysterious disappearance,
or possible continuation of Rome's lost Legion.
Paperback: 978-1-84694-559-5 ebook: 978-1-84694-931-9

Beaten But Not Defeated
Siegfried Moos - A German anti-Nazi who settled in
Britain Merilyn Moos
Siegi Moos, an anti-Nazi and active member of the German
Communist Party, escaped Germany in 1933 and, exiled
in Britain, sought another route to the transformation of
capitalism.
Paperback: 978-1-78279-677-0 ebook: 978-1-78279-676-3

A Schoolboy's Wartime Letters
An evacuee's life in WWII — A Personal Memoir
Geoffrey Iley
A boy writes home during WWII, revealing his own
fascinating story, full of zest for life, information and humour.
Paperback: 978-1-78279-504-9 ebook: 978-1-78279-503-2

The Life & Times of the Real Robyn Hoode
Mark Olly
A journey of discovery. The chronicles of the genuine
historical character, Robyn Hoode, and how he became
one of England's greatest legends.
Paperback: 978-1-78535-059-7 ebook: 978-1-78535-060-3